The Fine Art
of Flower Arranging

the fine art

A GARDEN CLUB OF AMERICA BOOK

# of flower arranging

TEXT BY NANCY D'OENCH

COORDINATION BY BONNY MARTIN

PHOTOGRAPHY BY MICK HALES

HARRY N. ABRAMS, INC., PUBLISHERS
in association with
THE GARDEN CLUB OF AMERICA

Project Director: Margai
Editors: Constance Hern
Designer: Helene Silverr
Photo Editor: John K. Cr
Production Manager: Al

Library of Congress Cata

D'Oench, Nancy.
   The fine art of flower a
photography by Mick Ha
   p. cm.
"A Garden Club of Amer
Includes bibliographical references (p.   ).
   ISBN 0-8109-3281-4
1. Flower arrangement. I. Garden Club of America. II. Title.
SB449 .D64 2002
745.92–dc21

2002006054

Printed and bound in China
10 9 8 7 6 5 4 3

Harry N. Abrams, Inc.
100 Fifth Avenue
New York, N.Y. 10011
www.abramsbooks.com

Abrams is a subsidiary of

Preceding spread: LINE IN MINIATURE *Julie Lapham*
This two-inch miniature exhibits all the characteristics one would find in a large-scale traditional line design.
It has an open silhouette influenced by Japanese flower arranging; the element of line predominates; and the
amount of material is restrained.
   A branch of Harry Lauder's walking stick, daisylike matricaria, and a bit of ivy are tucked into a tiny, glazed,
terra-cotta container. A rusty car part picked up from a gutter serves as the base and balances the "heavy"
branch at the top.

Overleaf: SOGETSU FREESTYLE *Gail Emmons*
Ikebana, the Japanese art of flower arranging, has influenced contemporary styles for flower shows and the home.
Line, enclosed space, and boldly contrasting forms and colors contribute to the drama of this freestyle design.

Contents

FOREWORD

THE PURPOSE OF *The Fine Art of Flower Arranging* is to help the reader develop an appreciation for the art of flower arranging. The artists' tools are neither paint nor bronze. Rather, as gardeners and advocates for our natural world, these artists have chosen to express themselves through plants.

This book showcases creations by some of the top flower arrangers in America today. We are indebted to them for giving freely of their talents and their time to produce these extraordinary arrangements, encompassing styles from the traditional to the modern. These designers are the best of the best. Beginning and experienced flower arrangers can hone their skills by studying the designs between these covers. They are the teaching tools of flower arranging, generously shared by their creators.

Two gifted arrangers, Nancy D'Oench of the Middletown Garden Club, Connecticut, and Bonny Martin of the Memphis Garden Club, Tennessee, conceived the idea of producing *The Fine Art of Flower Arranging* during Jan Pratt's term (1995–97) as president of the Garden Club of America. The work continued during the terms of the next three presidents—Chris Willemsen, Bobbie Hansen, and Ann Frierson. D'Oench and Martin traveled across the country attending flower shows in the company of talented photographer Mick Hales whose stunningly beautiful pictures speak for themselves. His masterful photography will preserve these preeminent examples of this ephemeral art for which there can be no museum.

Opposite, see *Exploration and Discovery*, page 98.

The first stated purpose of the Garden Club of America is "to stimulate the knowledge and love of gardening." Flower shows accomplish this goal in the most pleasant ways. Who has not been enthralled by the beauty and perfection of the flowers themselves and by the skill and artistry of the arrangers? We cannot overestimate the educational value of a well-planned and carefully executed flower show. Exhibitors and those who work behind the scenes, writing schedules, staging, clerking, and tending to hundreds of details, deserve our thanks. Dedicated and knowledgeable judges keep show standards high.

The Garden Club of America is proud to present this publication. We are grateful to Nancy D'Oench and Bonny Martin for producing it and to all who contributed to its success. We hope you will learn from *The Fine Art of Flower Arranging* and enjoy your journey to flower shows across the country.

BOBBIE HANSEN
President, Garden Club of America, 1999–2001
ANN FRIERSON
President, Garden Club of America, 2001–2003

INTRODUCTION

"A flower is relatively small. Everyone has many associations with a flower—the idea of flowers. You put out your hand to touch a flower—lean forward to smell it—maybe touch it with your lips almost without thinking—or give it to someone to please them. Still—in a way—nobody sees a flower—really it is so small—we haven't time—and to see takes time, like to have a friend takes time. If I could paint the flower exactly as I see it no one would see what I see because I would paint it small like the flower is small.

"So I said to myself—I'll paint what I see—what the flower is to me but I'll paint it big and they will be surprised into taking time to look at it—I will make even busy New Yorkers take time to see what I see of flowers." —Georgia O'Keeffe, 1939

Georgia O'Keeffe painted flowers on a large scale to make people stop and really look at them; we arrange flowers for the same reason. Whether the arrangement is an opulent Dutch period piece, a naturalistic ikebana design, or a Minimalist interpretation, the goal of an arranger is to focus the viewer's eye on the plant material. We select a piece of nature—whether an orchid from Thailand or a skunk cabbage from the swamp—and present it, arranged in such a way that viewers and we hope readers of this book will pause and see what we see. This is our art, just as painting was O'Keeffe's.

Merely placing a skunk cabbage blossom in a glass of water on the kitchen counter would be a step toward getting people to notice it. Some, who have never seen this sign of spring in the March mud, would wonder what it was; others might question what plans you had for it in terms of that night's menu. Sitting there, it is an interesting horticultural specimen. Arrangers believe it can be more, that they can add another dimension—their own sense of design and expression of creativity—and turn this specimen into a work of art, a flower arrangement. A low glazed container, for example, would emphasize the glossy surface and sculptural form of the skunk cabbage. The line of a budded branch would introduce contrast and still speak of spring. A few leaves at the base and water in the container could complete the picture. In the same location, on the kitchen counter, would more people stop and really see the flower? Try it.

Creative expression is a basic human need, suppressed in some, fulfilled in others. Flower arranging offers the artist in all of us an accessible and beautiful medium with which to express our innate creativity—on the kitchen counter at home or on a pedestal in a flower show. Flowers, arranged or not, have a universal appeal. Who does not respond to the indefinable quality of a blossom, the magic of nature? A Neanderthal grave

TIDAL WAVES
Phoebe Kahl and
Diana Rupp-Kennedy

In the arrangement, opposite, just two types of plant material-protea blossoms and New Zealand flax leaves-have been employed. They are interesting in their own right, the blossoms unusual, the leaves long and flexible. But, in the hands of the arrangers, the materials become the clay of this sculptural art form.

A flower show asked entrants for an interpretation of "tidal waves." The story of the sea's ebb and flow begins in the ceramic container with its rising and falling loops. This motion is echoed in the flax leaves, manipulated to enclose space and to bring the eye back to the protea blossoms' upward facing petals, which start the movement once again. The container, proteas, and flax leaves all share a linear pattern which unifies the design, while the blossoms add a contrasting punch of color. The composition is anchored to the pedestal by stones ground smooth by the sea's currents.

dating back 46,000 years revealed large quantities of flower pollen, evidence that very early humans valued the ephemeral beauty of blooms and possibly used them as a token of affection or esteem for the deceased. Perhaps science will reveal that somewhere in our DNA chains there is a marker for "flower response." If so, it will only confirm what we have sensed all along.

In *Design in Flower Arrangement* (1937) the artist John Taylor Arms wrote, "We cannot all be Shakespeares, or Rembrandts, or Beethovens, but we can be truly and fully ourselves, expressing our emotions, as they expressed theirs, through a chosen medium. Nor can we all possess such a well-defined talent, nor so arrange our lives, that the medium be engraving, or painting, or music or sculpture. But all of us have access to flowers— fragile, changing, pliable, provoking, colorful, exquisite." By understanding design as it applies to all art, Arms wrote, we can express beauty through flowers. "Beauty," he added, "has the power to lift us from our lower to our higher selves and surely, the world was never more in need of this than now."

In the first section of this book we explore how the art of flower arranging has responded historically to creative forces in Western and Eastern civilizations, and how these forces are reflected in the way we use the flowers from our gardens in our homes and public places. In the second section we see the two influences converge, then emerge in the new art that is on exhibit in flower shows today. Through these images and through the arrangers' words, we hope to communicate the very real allure of flower arranging, what it is that makes arrangers arrange.

The arrangers whose designs are featured in this book strive to create works of art out of plant material because they have discovered the pleasures of the creative process. They enjoy the stimulus and challenge of a design in process, an arrangement taking shape in the back of the mind. Once the enthusiasm for creating flower arrangements takes hold no walk in the woods or drive along an interstate highway is without its rewards. The curve of a branch, the texture of a fungus, the silhouette of a building may have gone unnoticed before but now are seen for their design qualities. These images may well be called up for use in producing future flower arrangements.

We hope to pass on a bit of this artistic enthusiasm to you the reader, to open eyes, to show the rewards of this art form. As you pause to study the arrangements, we believe you will find fresh ways of presenting the flowers that we all love so that visitors to your home or event will stop, look, and really see the flowers. Flower arranging encompasses the art of seeing—for the arranger and the viewer.

NANCY D'OENCH

Opposite: Garden flowers, beautifully arranged, grace the hallway of Cecile McCaull's Connecticut home. For more on gardeners who arrange and arrangers who garden, see pages 46-67.

Our Flower-Arranging Heritage

VICTORIAN IN SPIRIT

Manisse K. Newell

Twenty-one different kinds of blossoms are skillfully massed into a silver Georgian epergne that belonged to the arranger's great-grandmother. Here is a tribute to the era of grand Victorian gardens and the love of nature that brought its bounty into the parlor.

No single flower or color stands out. Instead, all the forms and textures create an embroidered effect. Compact and opulent, wider than high, it is the lushness of texture that conveys the Victorian taste. The rounded forms—peonies, lilies, roses, alliums, lilacs, hydrangeas, viburnums, carnations, lisianthuses, and campanulas— are joined by the more linear foxgloves, snapdragons, stock, delphiniums, and grevilleas.

The handsome composition is displayed in an equally opulent setting, atop the grand piano in the ballroom at Filoli.

Every flower arrangement that is created today—whether it contains a single blossom in a simple bud vase or hundreds of stems in a towering arrangement for a grand opening—is the product of two inspirations. The originality of the arranger is of primary importance, but the centuries of floral design that have gone before carry tremendous weight as well. Our flower arrangements reflect what flowers have meant and how they have been used through the ages, the accumulated experience of our cultural heritage. This heritage, in turn, is shaped by two distinct traditions—flower arranging in the Western world and flower arranging in Japan.

For hundred of years each of these two cultures has treated flower arranging very differently. Only in the twentieth century did the two come closer together, each incorporating qualities of the other tradition.

In *The Art of Arranging Flowers: A Complete Guide to Japanese Ikebana* (1966), Shozo Sato summarized the difference in the two approaches to flower arranging this way: "In the Occidental world, flowers are used as decorations on a level with curtains, slip covers, and lamp shades, and in the past have followed the style prevailing in other arts of their time—whether Egyptian, Classical, Renaissance, Baroque, Rococo, Romantic, or Abstract. In Japan, flower arrangements are also used as decorations, but on a level with paintings and other art objects."

Flower arranging is definitely an art in Japan today, as it has been for hundreds of years, but its practice is not restricted to "artists." Men and women, children and adults, soldiers and sumo wrestlers all find satisfaction in its study and practice.

In the following chapters we review the Western tradition, look closely at the history and art of ikebana, and examine how flowers have come to be part of a beautifully decorated interior. We show how the two styles have been integrated, often unconsciously, into the styles of arrangement we use in our homes today. Both traditions reflect the urge to bring the garden indoors, and in Chapter 3 we visit four very special gardens and observe how the treasures that grow there are transformed into the art known as flower arranging.

Chapter 1

Flower Arranging in the West—
A Very Long Tradition

Through the ages, Occidental flower arranging has reflected the styles and trends of architecture and the decorative arts. It has also represented the economic, political, and religious climate of the era—with restraint and symbolism in religious times, with exuberance and opulence in prosperous times.

It is not always easy to document traditions of arranging that are centuries old. Typically the researcher must rely on the art and literature of the day, recognizing that the time frames labeled as "periods" represent decades of ever-changing fashion and that a designation may cover many countries and sometimes even continents. When we add to these variables the fact that arrangers then, as now, had their own individual styles, we realize that the person who hopes to do an arrangement today in the spirit of a period has a great deal of leeway.

In this chapter, we feature arrangements with some of the characteristics of historic periods. These designs show how Western flower arranging has assimilated elements of style from the preceding 400 years, even 4,500 years, and adapted them for use in our homes and public spaces today. The study of historical eras, from that of the ancient Egyptians onward, reveals something about the way flowers were used and in fact can inspire us with design ideas for today. Covering the floor to a depth of two feet with roses, as the Romans did, may not be a desirable addition to the next dinner party, but a garland of foliage and flowers running the length of the table is a definite possibility. In this brief review of flower-arranging history and in the arrangements that follow is evidence that this art form is not static, that it retains much of the past, that it responds to current fashions, and that it continues to explore new means of expression.

We begin our exploration of Western flower arranging forty-five centuries ago in the region of the Nile River and then briefly examine how each era has employed flowers and plant material—first in ceremonial life and later at home.

EGYPTIAN (c. 2700–1069 B.C.E.)

If we define *flower arranging* as placing cut flowers in a container, we are able to trace the art and practice of flower arranging back about 4,500 years to the Old Kingdom in ancient Egypt during Dynasty 5, now dated about 2510–2460 B.C.E. In her book *Period*

Flower Arrangement (1953), Margaret Fairbanks Marcus featured a fragment from Perneb's tomb that is at the Metropolitan Museum of Art. Carved in relief on stone are water lilies, buds, and lily pads, set at regular intervals around the rim of a wide-mouthed basin. This simple arrangement is marked by order and clarity, repetition and alteration, qualities found in many other forms of Egyptian art, including the collars of flowers and leaves seen in the costumes of the day. More formal bouquets of lotus and other flowers were offered to the dead or presented to the gods. Floral artists were expert at threading blossoms or fruit into other flowers, thus creating a compound form. The Egyptians enjoyed the bounty that the Nile Valley offered.

GREEK (c. 600–146 B.C.E.)

The records of everyday life in ancient Greece yield little evidence of cut flowers in vases; instead, flowers were fashioned into chaplets—wreaths for the head—and garlands. Indeed, there seems to have been a wreath for every occasion. Wreath and garland makers were the florists of the day with wealthier households employing their own. One house is said to have maintained a staff of more than forty just to meet the demands for wreaths and garlands.

During this era books were written about the proper flowers to be used for each kind of wreath. Funeral wreaths, for example, could include roses, narcissus, and sweet marjoram; each god was identified with a favorite flower at festivals and in temples. There were wreaths for athletes and wreaths for a suitor to hang on the door of his beloved. Even today we retain a number of associations that date back to the symbolism possessed by plant material in Greek tradition. The laurel wreath still suggests victory; the olive branch, peace; the rose, love. Roses were also the symbol of secrecy, an idea that carried into the Middle Ages when white roses hung from the ceiling meant that whatever happened beneath was secret . . .sub rosa.

IMPERIAL ROMAN (28 B.C.E.–330 C.E.)

The Romans embraced and embellished the art of wreath and garland making. Wreaths became more crownlike, rising to a point above the forehead; garlands were more dramatic, wider in the center and tapering. Wealth and power were reflected in the lavish, even ostentatious use of flowers. At banquets, the floor would be strewn not just with a few rose petals but with flowers two feet deep. Lilies, hyacinths, and narcissus would rain from the ceiling.

A second-century Roman mosaic at the Vatican Museums is the earliest record we have of a Western-style bouquet in a container. This image of a basket of flowers was found near Tivoli at Hadrian's Villa and contains a delightful arrangement of mixed flowers— roses, anemones, tulips and carnations, morning glories and hyacinths. Larger flowers drop over the rim of the basket; smaller flowers have been placed at the top; tendrils of vine form graceful curves, enclosing voids. Colors range from red to rose to pink, with touches of pale yellow, blue, and white. This early example of Western flower arranging could well grace a table or terrace today.

EARLY BYZANTINE (312–867)

In 330 C.E., Emperor Constantine the Great chose Byzantium, the ancient Greek city on the Bosporus, to be the site of the new capital of the Roman Empire and renamed the city Constantinople. When the Roman Empire was split into western and eastern sections, Constantinople served as the capital of what was generally called the Eastern Roman Empire, 395–476. (The empire, eventually called the Byzantine Empire, lasted until the Turks captured Constantinople in 1453.) For many centuries, Constantinople stood not only as a protector of its Greek heritage and the Roman style of government but also as the center of the Christian religion. It also controlled the trade routes from east to west and north to south. The confluence of cultures produced the first golden age of Byzantine art, examples of which are preserved in the mosaics at the Church of the Hagia Sophia (532–37) in Constantinople and in the Byzantine churches of Italy, such as the Church of San Vitale (c. 547) and the Church of Sant'Apollinare in Classe (533–49). Stylized trees that appear in the earlier Christian Imperial mosaics of the Mausoleum of Galla Placida (c. 425–26) in Ravenna, Italy, have become one of the most recognizable floral compositions from this age. Tall, slim, symmetrical spires rise from ornate urns or baskets, the foliage accented with flowers or fruit at regular intervals. Sometimes a narrow ribbon traces a path from the base to the top.

This flower-arranging style taken from the ancient mosaics has inspired the cones of plant material that today decorate formal buffet tables, sideboards, hall tables, and mantels, especially during the holiday season.

GOTHIC (c. 1200–c. 1485)

To learn how flowers were arranged in any given period, historians must rely, in large part, on the visual arts. From the fall of the Western Roman Empire in the fifth century to the dawn of the Renaissance in the fifteenth, flowers, wreaths, and bouquets must have had a place at banquets and festivities, but they were seldom represented in the art of the day. Instead, the art of the period was primarily a reflection of religious belief, and when flowers did appear, it was usually as religious symbolism.

In the Italian city of Siena, the center panel of an altarpiece, *Annunciation*, painted for the Siena Cathedral by the fourteenth-century artist Simone Martini, shows a gold vase with four stems of tall, stately Madonna lilies sitting on the floor between Mary and the angel Gabriel. The lily symbolized purity and fertility and appeared in many frescoes as the Virgin's flower. Sometimes the tall stalks of lilies were circled with short-stemmed roses, ferns, or lilies-of-the-valley. Other paintings in and around Siena show the Virgin with sprays of roses rising to twice or even three times the height of the container. This simple style of dramatic proportions is an effective one for altar flowers even today.

RENAISSANCE (c. 1400–c. 1600)

"The Renaissance was heir to many traditions," Marcus reminds us in *Period Flower*

Arrangement. "Byzantine splendor, Greek and Roman forms, and symbolism from both the classical and Christian worlds contributed to the flower arrangements of the time."

In Hugo van der Goes's *Adoration of the Shepherds*, the central panel of the *Portinari Altarpiece* (c. 1474–76), the Virgin is the primary focus, but flowers appear in the foreground and are painted with botanical accuracy. The fifteenth-century viewer would recognize the swordlike leaves of the iris as symbols of death; the deep orange lilies standing for blood; the blue iris as emblems of heaven and goodness. Violets strewn on the ground would recall the Christian legend that these flowers grew in the shadow of the Cross and drooped in mourning when Jesus died. A clear glass, denoting purity, holds a stem of columbine with seven fully opened blossoms, representing the seven gifts of the Holy Spirit — wisdom, understanding, counsel, strength, knowledge, true godliness, and holy fear.

In the background of the *Borghese Virgin* (c. 1500), by a follower of Botticelli, there are two pedestal vases that appear to be about four feet tall. If we were to re-create these arrangements today, we might use ornate, carved candlesticks fitted with saucers of Oasis at the top. Flowers such as roses would be placed in a loose pyramid form, some sprays falling over the sides. The result would be much like the table centerpieces often used today for weddings and large parties, arrangements that create a dramatic impression as guests enter the room, but do not interfere with the line of vision or conversation across the table once the diners are seated.

BAROQUE (c. 1575–c. 1775)

In the art of the periods we have just reviewed, religious or allegorical figures were the main focus; flowers were incidental. Four hundred years ago, in the Baroque period, that changed. The real story of Western flower arranging begins there.

In the magnificent paintings by the Dutch and Flemish artists of the seventeenth and eighteenth centuries—Jan Brueghel the Elder, Ambrosius Bosschaert, Jan van Huysum, P. T. van Brussel, Jan van Os, and others—flowers took center stage.

It is tempting to think of the grand bouquets in these flower paintings as decorating the reception area of a Flemish mansion or the center of a Dutch banquet table. We know that this is not the case. Some paintings of the period do show flowers in the home, but they are modest arrangements. In *Concordia* by Marten de Vos a mantel bouquet is part of a contented family scene. *The Happy Family* by Jan Steen shows a merry gathering with food, wine, music, and a vase of flowers in the background. These are not the lavish displays that come to mind when we think of the Dutch flower piece. Those extravagant arrangements were not composed to decorate a home or even a large hall. They had another purpose.

This was a time of great prosperity and speculation in Holland, of exploration and passionate collecting. A flower painting such as Jan van Huysum's *Flowers Piece* (1726), now in the Wallace Collection, London, featuring a terra-cotta container overflowing with primroses, fritillaries, poppies, tulips, roses, peonies, narcissi, hyacinths, a crown-imperial,

BAROQUE IN SPIRIT
Lou Greer

This opulent arrangement, reminiscent of a Dutch flower piece, features an array of distinctive plant material, each variety vying for center stage. Most typical of the Baroque style, perhaps, are the parrot tulips with their arching stems, some facing the viewer, others turned away. A large full allium claims the uppermost position, but just as compelling are the single coral peonies, the lilies, and the irises.

Each flower—delphinium, Queen Anne's lace, scabiosa, dianthus, shrub rose—is interesting in its own right, its beauty recalling the "flower portraits" of the seventeenth century when patrons commissioned artists such as Justus van Huysum of Holland to record the botanical treasures that bloomed during the year in their greenhouses.

The bird's nest is a frequent feature in Baroque-era flower paintings, as is the recessed setting. This niche is in the entrance to Filoli.

butterflies, moths, and a bird's nest with eggs—would tell the contemporary viewer much about the person who commissioned it. Flowers were the preserve of the well-to-do. These flower paintings were deliberate, even ostentatious displays of wealth, power, and sophistication. An informed observer would know how much each seed or bulb had cost, where it had come from, and the clever negotiations required to win such a rare specimen. The flower paintings were the seventeenth-century version of conspicuous consumption. (Indeed, the Dutch word for these paintings was *pronkstilleven*, which translates as "show-off still lifes.")

Even the casual horticulturist will recognize that all of the flowers in these paintings could not have bloomed at the same time. A flower painting was a year's worth of wonders from the garden and the greenhouse contained on one canvas or wood panel. It was also insurance against the possibility that one or more of those wonders might not perform next year.

While the horticulturist sees the impossibility of all those flowers blooming at the same time, the flower arranger recognizes that even if they did, it would be difficult if not impossible to arrange them as they appear in some of the paintings. The artist has let neither gravity nor stem length dictate where each blossom is placed.

How, then, did the artist put these compositions together? One clue might be found in the writing of Gérard de Lairesse, a Dutch printer, etcher, engraver, and art theorist of the time. Paul Taylor in *Dutch Flower Painting, 1600–1720* (1995) quoted this advice from Lairesse to artists: "Paint all sorts of flowers on pieces of card or cardboard . . .; make five or six of each colour, . . . red, blue, purple, yellow, mauve, or violet, but six of each. . . Besides these make smaller ones. . . . Cut all these apart, and place each color in an orderly manner in little boxes. Then paint a green Festoon or Bouquet on a plank or on cardboard, complete with foliage; on which you can place such flower as you want, arranging and rearranging them in accordance with your thoughts. . . ."

Flower arrangers will recognize another tip from Lairesse as something they have done while working out the placement of plant material in a design. During the winter months, Lairesse advises, artists should collect paper and silk flowers on wire stalks, in all colors, and use them to practice, seeing how one color and form works against another.

In his book *Het groot Schilderboeck* (1707), Lairesse named qualities that are essential for a good flower painting. The first requirement is that the flowers themselves be selected for their excellence of size, beauty, and esteem, "and there should be none which are poor or common." In other words, Lairesse wanted to see choice cultivars, no roadside weeds or ordinary garden flowers. A second criterion refers to "good arrangement and harmony," stressing the point that "the most beautiful and noble flowers" be displayed in the most prominent position. And third, Lairesse wanted "each flower to be well expressed according to its nature and quality."

The best paintings in this genre clearly follow his advice. A spectacular crown-imperial fritillary or Madonna lily, for instance, will stand high in the design with every other specimen given its own space and represented with botanical accuracy.

FRENCH AND ROCOCO (c. 1715–c. 1774)

In contrast to the opulence of the Dutch arrangements, the French style is characterized as light, airy, graceful, and delicately elegant. The bold S-curve used in many flower pieces of the Baroque era gives way in the Rococo period to a gentler C-curve. Each flower still has its space, and the stems show, holding the flower heads aloft. There is harmony like in the soft coloring of an Aubusson rug rather than bold contrast. Arrangers might think of a pretty, essentially feminine room with gilded French chairs and a writing table. The arrangement can reflect this spirit and gaiety through scale, line, and color.

French in Spirit
Carolyn Musto

In a marble font in the portico to Filoli, a Rococo urn holds an airy French-style arrangement of pastel-colored garden flowers. In the soft colors of an Aubusson rug, the pinks of peony tulips, foxgloves, coral bells, and roses—Eden, Martin Guillot, Baby Blanket, and Mint Julep—are set off by the blues of scabiosas, delphiniums, Canterbury bells, and sweet peas. Eucharist lilies add a sparkle of white.

Balanced but not quite symmetrical and taller than it is wide, this design has a lively, feminine feeling. Each blossom has its own space, and stems are allowed to show. A variety of blossoms in a limited palette has been arranged to create a light and elegant design.

GEORGIAN (C. 1720–C. 1780)

Even if we limit our focus to England and North America during the eighteenth century, we still have a period with as many faces as there are flowers in a mass arrangement. Some sources divide these six decades into early and late English Georgian, American Georgian, and Williamsburg. During these years Dutch, Italian, and French influences, as well as new imports from China, affected the fashions of the day. The earlier Georgian arrangements retained much of the Dutch influence, whereas later Georgian resembled the lighter French style. According to Marcus, "All Georgian arrangements should have a certain formal grandeur, but there may be variants of the style." Other writers have recommended symmetrical balance, a triangular shape in which the whole is more important than individual flowers, and a harmonious color scheme.

Flower arranging in North America during the same period varied widely depending on the background and circumstances of the settlers. New England Puritans of necessity concentrated on medicinal and culinary herbs. The Dutch in New Amsterdam had a slightly milder climate and brought their bulbs and flower seeds with them. The English settlers in Williamsburg had a climate still more conducive to growing flowers and were influenced in their garden design and flower arranging by the prevailing styles in England.

GEORGIAN IN SPIRIT
Ellie Gardner

This harmonious design in the formal Georgian spirit looks right at home atop a painted commode in the oak-paneled study at Filoli. The flowers blend into a harmonious whole that is more important than the individual flower. A linear larkspur, at the apex of the triangle, prescribes the design's dimensions and is supported by snapdragons, bells of Ireland, asparagus fern, and quince branches around the perimeter. Roses, lilies, gerberas, and tulips fill in the picture.

Flowers fall gracefully over the rim of the container, merging the gray of urn with the pinks in the arrangement.

FEDERAL AND NEOCLASSICAL (c. 1780–c. 1830)

The classical revival of the late eighteenth and early nineteenth centuries changed the face of decoration across Europe, in England, and in North America. Symmetry and straight lines, inspired by the ornamentation in the recently excavated cities of Pompeii and Herculaneum—which had been buried during the 79 c.e. eruption of Mount Vesuvius—replaced the Rococo curves of an earlier era.

The spirit of the Federal period can be suggested in flower arrangments by symmetrical, massed designs that are nonetheless somewhat open, with the beauty of the individual flower still stressed. In tall vases of classical design, the height of the composition should be greater than the width, suggesting a slim elegance. Low basins and boat-shaped bowls may also be used to hold low mounds of flowers and foliage, simulating carved mantel decorations. Harmony of color rather than vivid contrasts is a hallmark of the Neoclassical style.

FEDERAL IN SPIRIT
Margaret Lee Blunt

A three-part silver epergne lifts this mounded Federal design and gives it a lightness in spite of the wealth of plant material. The matched curves of lupine accentuate the formal symmetrical balance and suggest carved mantel decoration. Here in the dining room at Filoli, they also mirror the figures in the tapestry.

Peonies in pinks and deep reds, and roses in yellows, peaches, and pinks—combined with the purple of sweet peas, the green of young apples, and the blue spikes of veronica—create a mass arrangement that is harmonious and open enough to show the beauty of individual flowers. Eucharist lilies, newly arrived on the market from New Zealand, add a crisp white form.

The dishes of the epergne are lined with plastic to protect the silver, then filled with Oasis. A light covering of moss helps retain moisture.

VICTORIAN AND ROMANTIC (c. 1830–c. 1890)

The rigorous symmetry and delicate furniture of the Federal period gave way in the mid to late nineteenth century to the elaborate decoration we associate with the Victorian era. Flower arrangements in this period reflected a love of the color, forms, and personalities of plants. Specimens with bizarre markings were favored as they were in Dutch paintings, but instead of setting each flower apart, the Victorian arranger massed the blossoms together, creating an overall effect suggesting rich embroidery, as illustrated on page 13. Flowers were low and mounded, perhaps half the height of the container. Bold color contrasts were popular but so were all-white arrangements.

The designs on this and the following page show the richness of textures and patterns favored in the Victorian period. The photographs were taken in the Victorian parlor of Bayou Bend, the former home of the Texas philanthropist and collector, Ima Hogg.

In 1930 Hogg began building an extensive collection of art and antiques that would tell the story of America's taste, style, and customs from colonial times to the Victorian era. In 1966 the Bayou Bend Collection, known as the American Wing of the Museum of Fine Arts, Houston, was opened to the public. Since then members of the River Oaks Garden Club have decorated each room on a weekly basis with fresh flower arrangements appropriate to the period.

VICTORIAN IN SPIRIT
Carol Ballard and Laura Wheless

Ornate describes this Victorian parlor with its carved marble mantel, embossed tea service, gilt clock, candlesticks, and gold-framed mirror. The flowers offer a welcome note of freshness. On the marble table, an etched-glass container with a pierced silver rim holds a tight cluster of spring narcissi, hyacinths, sweet peas, and red roses, gentled at the edges with maidenhair fern. The tea service was available from Tiffany & Co. in the 1850s.

The pair of vases on the mantel date from about the same period and depict Uncle Tom, Little Eva, and Eliza with her baby from *Uncle Tom's Cabin.* They hold monkshood from the cutting garden at Bayou Bend and flank a French clock sold in St. Louis about 1870.

VICTORIAN IN SPIRIT
Carol Ballard and Laura Wheless

A white hydrangea centered by the palest pink rose is tucked into a Victorian nosegay holder, creating an accessory worthy of a bride or a prom queen. A pincushion and an ivory case for needlework equipment are nearby. Perhaps a daughter might breathe in the rose's fragrance in between stitches and while listening to guests' conversation. The flowers in the tussy mussy could also convey a silent message to a visitor, for in the Victorian language of flowers a rose expressed love.

TRADITIONAL MASS DESIGNS

In the twentieth century, the tightly packed masses of the Victorian era gave way to a more open and flexible style known as the traditional mass arrangement. Distinguishing characteristics of previous periods were freely employed but with modern modifications. It is still a popular look and remains the style of choice for many homes, places of worship, and public buildings.

The three arrangements that follow can all be classified as traditional mass, even though they differ widely in color, shape, and selection of plant material. They share common characteristics that in no way limit variation or originality. On the contrary, experience has shown that these qualities guarantee that a finished design will possess stable balance, good scale, and pleasing proportion, freeing the arranger to apply his or her own personal stamp.

The following is a list of characteristics common to traditional mass arrangements. The reader might examine these three designs to see how these qualities have been incorporated:

- A focal area appears near the base of the arrangement in the boldest, brightest blossoms.

- From the focal area, the plant material is selected for its size and intensity of color to make a gradual transition to the finest forms on the perimeter of the design. One alliterative way to describe this gradation is "big, bright blossoms at the bottom moving to petite forms and pale colors on the periphery."

- Some material falls over the edge of the container. This unifies the design by breaking the horizontal line of the rim, which would otherwise divide the design into flowers on top and container on the bottom.

- All lines appear to rise from a single point but are angled to create a sense of depth and balance.

- The plant material is at least one and a half times the height plus the width of the container, and sometimes much taller.

TRADITIONAL MASS DESIGN
Cary Lide

Coral lilies and pale-peach roses and tulips begin the monochromatic palette for this traditional mass arrangement with elements of Georgian grandeur. Closed lily buds, stock, and snapdragons aid the transition from the round forms of the open lilies and roses to the linear larkspurs that edge the design.

This elegant arrangement sits atop a pedestal in a niche of the dining room at Rienzi, the former home of Harris and Carol Masterson. The house was recently opened to the public as the European decorative arts wing of the Museum of Fine Arts, Houston. The oriental bowl that holds the arrangement is from Rienzi's porcelain collection.

TRADITIONAL MASS DESIGN
Diane Dalton and Kitty Ferguson

Framed by an arch at the Tower Hill Botanic Garden in Boylston, Massachusetts, this regal mass arrangement could grace the reception area of a stately home, or an alcove in a cathedral. The cone shape suggests the stylized trees of Byzantium, but the compactness of the design and strong contrasts reflect the Victorian aesthetic.

Coral roses catch the viewer's attention and start a visual path from the base of the design upward. The changing angle of the roses, from full frontal to upward facing, defines the direction. Along the way they are joined by white roses leading to the foxtail lilies. Bells of Ireland reinforce the linear forms at the top and are used again to curve over the edge of the urn.

Lilies in a deeper shade of coral provide a contrast in shape, as do the dahlias placed deeper into the design. Dill and lady's-mantle lighten the composition with their airy forms and yellow-green color, while blue lisianthus makes the perfect triad complement to the corals and greens already there.

This traditional mass design is an exercise in symmetrical balance and color contrasts.

TRADITIONAL MASS DESIGN
Martha Newton Law

This traditional mass design artfully combines the best of several periods—the airiness and subtle palette of the French period, the grandeur and harmony of the Georgian, and the classical elegance of the Federal.

The bold form of the amaryllis blossom leaves no doubt where the focal area of this traditional mass is. A medley of pink and white—deep pink tulips, white azaleas, snapdragons, and larkspurs—moves from the central amaryllis blossoms out to the fringes of spirea and pussy willow. Held aloft in a classical urn, the tulip stems and sweeping branches continue the movement begun in the curve of the container's handles. There is nothing static in this design—even the large amaryllis blossoms seem to waltz from lower left to upper right.

This classic springtime arrangement in pink, white, and green is evidence of why the traditional mass style remains a much-loved and ever popular form. Here it graces the entrance to the Hunt and Polo Club in Memphis.

MASSED-LINE ARRANGEMENTS

A variation of the traditional mass arrangement is the massed-line, an arrangement with a quantity of flowers and the suggestion of a Hogarth curve, a crescent, or other line direction, either vertical or horizontal. Space and setting can make this the style of choice.

MASSED-LINE ARRANGEMENT
Anne Helfert

This full massed-line arrangement conforms to the horizontal space below the tapestry in the dining room at Filoli and captures the movement in the scene and the intricacy of the needlework. Garden roses—Eden, Brass Band, and Sally Holmes—join delphiniums, peonies, roses, rhododendrons, sweet peas, bells of Ireland, scabiosas, snapdragons, and lisianthuses in recalling the exuberance of Dutch designs.

The actions of the main characters in the tapestry engage the viewer, but then the eye moves around the composition —what is the dog about to examine; what is the figure on the left; who is in the background? Similarly, the intense palette of the arrangement attracts the viewer's attention with the eye drawn into the large central peony. But a longer look reveals a variety of forms and textures and the subtle variations of color.

This colorful bold design illustrates a current fashion in flower arranging known as modern mass. Each color or type of material is grouped or massed, with no transition between one and the next. The coral roses, for example, are placed next to the deep purples of rhododendrons, freesias, and lilacs for a bold contrast. Looped aspidistra leaves add another modern touch and suggest enclosed space even in this compact design. Here, apricots continue the warm tones of the roses and lilies but introduce a new shape and surface quality.

The container is a classical urn, and the overall silhouette and compactness of this arrangement are similar to the Victorian design on page 13, but because of the grouping and the limited variety of plant material, the look and feel of the design are entirely different.

MODERN MASS DESIGNS

While mass and massed-line arrangements remain popular forms of traditional design, other fashions in flower arranging are gaining widespread acceptance. In recent years the French and Italian schools of design have been influenced by innovative trends in ikebana to use masses of plant material in original ways. Styles that are bold, dynamic, and sculptural have evolved. One of these, the modern mass design, is characterized by masses of plant material in one variety and color, juxtaposed with a mass in a contrasting color and texture. Fruit, a bold form and a new texture, is frequently incorporated, as is a strong curved branch or other form to add line to the mass of the central design. The result is dramatic. Many arrangers find this style more easily achieved than the traditional mass arrangement with its graduated transitions.

Hawaiian Modern
Arrangement by Bertie Lee, home of Claire and Larry Johnson

An armload of Blue Giant agapanthus, cut from a friend's garden, arranged by another friend, and massed in the modern European style, adorns the dining room table of this home on the island of Oahu, Hawaii. Seed pods from spider lilies give stability to the design and offer contrast, as do the miniature green ti leaves and clipped rhapis palm. White spathiphyllum blossoms float out from the base, adding an airy touch while balancing the compact, towering cluster.

On a table in the entry way, visible at left, is a vase of pink ginger blossoms (*Alpinia purpurata*, 'Jungle Queen'). These were cut from the Johnsons' garden, which is known for its collection of gingers. Claire Johnson says, "We all go into each other's gardens. If we want agapanthus, we go to Stephanie Lee's garden; that's where Bertie Lee got the flowers for the arrangement on the dining room table. If arrangers want ginger, they come here."

To the right a silver service is complemented by a white moth orchid (*Phalaenopsis*).

TABLE DECOR

Center of Attention
Arrangement by Ann Stevens, home of Ann and John Tatum

The low, rounded form of the Federal, Victorian, and modern mass designs is often adapted for the contemporary table. Here a rounded but airy arrangement in corals and yellows is the centerpiece for a dinner party. The botanical art in the center of the green-rimmed dinner plates is enlarged and intensified in the bright coral lilies, yellow gerberas, blue delphiniums, and flowering plums of the centerpiece. A silver tureen, used as a container, adds its own elegant note to the engraved Rhine wine glasses, gold-rimmed goblets, and crisp linen.

Flowering branches on oriental wall panels continue the botanical theme, and a fern near the window contributes another luxuriant note to the dining room of the Tatum home in Savannah, Georgia.

Dutch Influence
Arrangement by Liz Farnsworth, home of Liz and Tommy Farnsworth

An alternative treatment to the table setting pictured to the left is seen above, at a table with all the exuberance of the Baroque period. Guests entering this room will be transported to enchanted realms by this floral cornucopia held aloft by an antique wood figure. Seated guests, however, will be able to converse easily, as the floriferous explosion is well above eye level.

The apricot walls with accents of soft green provide a harmonious background for this arrangement of tulips, ranunculuses, roses, orchids, lilies, hydrangeas, viburnums, spirea, and lilacs that exudes the lushness of a Dutch flower painting. The pinks, corals, reds, and golds of the flowers are repeated in the table—in the silk-rose napkin rings and the finely detailed crystal.

Dinner plates in black and gold echo the framing of the chair backs, and silver goblets, no two alike, keep the eye moving around the table, looking for even more surprises, such as the rose petals in the finger bowls.

Chapter 2 Ikebana–Ancient Art, Newest Influence

Ikebana, the Japanese art of flower arranging, traces its beginnings back to the sixth century, yet it is probably the major influence on flower arranging in both the East and West today. In this chapter we first look at the history and philosophy behind this Japanese art and then examine how it has evolved into the innovative style and leading influence that it is today.

Both Eastern and Western cultures celebrate the beauty of nature in their flower arranging, but they differ in basic concepts. Western flower arranging stems from the tradition of gardening and reflects the bounty and variety of the garden. Ikebana's origins were religious—the arrangements were made to decorate Buddhist altars—so its practitioners approach the art with more reverence. Students of ikebana also believe that it is possible to present a cut flower or branch so that it is even more beautiful than when it was growing in the garden.

Norman Sparnon, in *Creative Japanese Flower Arrangement*, (1982), explained this last element of ikebana: "The Ikebana arranger is not content just to see a beautiful flower growing. Instead, he wants to communicate the beauty and the meaning of the flower to others. It is the arranger's sensitivity to beauty, combined with an emotional urge toward creativeness, that can refine a natural design to the point where it transcends nature. . . . Effort must be made to read the minds of the plants; to go beyond their superficial botanical aspects and so to grasp the meaning of their being, spiritually as well as materially."

"Less is more," an aphorism used so often to express the restraint of ikebana, reminds the arranger to let each flower or branch have its moment, to experience each blossom to the fullest. Then and only then can the flower "speak," revealing its personality and spirituality to the arranger.

This communication between flower and arranger creates the feeling of *wa*—peace of the soul. Jane Morgan, a professor of the Ikenobo school of ikebana, has compared this feeling to the deep joy of the pianist, the sculptor, or the dirt gardener who becomes so immersed in his or her creative efforts that all outside distractions disappear. "It is almost a spiritual experience," she has said, "like that of the fisherman who 'goes to church' while casting into the ocean."

Morgan has studied in the United States and Japan and conducts workshops around the country. She has been an invaluable source of information for the following description of the history, philosophy, symbolism, and styles of ikebana.

Ikebana, she has pointed out, is more than an art, it is an expression of Asian philosophy that encompasses an adoration of nature, a reverence for creativity, and a quest for the spiritual. In ikebana, plant material is admired, not just for its form, color, and texture but also for what it represents—for its symbolism:

- Buds represent the future, with the anticipation of seeing them open.
- Luscious foliage and half-open flowers speak of the present.
- Dried leaves and seed pods foretell the end of the season.

Particular flowers suggest seasons:
- Irises are the symbol of spring.
- Morning glories symbolize summer.
- Chrysanthemums are the symbol for fall.
- Ivy signals regret at the oncoming desolation of winter.
- Dried lotus is the symbol of winter.

Human emotions, values, and virtues can all be interpreted by the flower selection:
- White roses are a symbol of purity.
- Red roses symbolize oneness.
- Tree peonies symbolize sensual pleasure.
- A weeping willow branch, tied in a loop, is a symbol of hospitality.

HOW IT ALL BEGAN

Symbolism goes back to the very beginning of ikebana, to its very heart. In the sixth century, priests returning to Japan from China introduced the custom of offering flowers to Buddha. Standing, upright flowers were placed on either side of Buddhist deities. While incense was considered food for the deities, flowers were a symbolic expression of adoration. The beautifully designed containers that we see in ancient drawings and that are still copied were introduced to hold these flower offerings.

By the fifteenth century the large altar arrangements were defined as *rikka*s. They had a unique, one-stemmed, trunklike effect rising above the waterline and contained either seven or nine materials that depicted landscapes. Branches and flowers represented the distant and near mountains, craggy waterfalls, villages, rivers, and streams.

In the sixteenth and seventeenth centuries *rikka*s became a full-fledged art and a pastime of nobles and warriors, gracing castles, the homes of nobility, and festivals.

Following the strict rules of construction, *rikka*s sometimes reached enormous sizes. The peak of massiveness, according to Norman Sparnon's *Japanese Flower Arrangement Classical and Modern* (1960), was possibly achieved in 1693 when two *rikka*s, forty feet high, were built for either side of the Great Buddha at Nara.

Although temples and castles could accommodate the stately *rikka*s, something smaller and less formal was required for the homes of the rising mercantile class. The *shoka*, a three-branched simplification of the *rikka*, evolved using one to three materials instead of the seven to nine. The three branches represented heaven, man, and earth. This style fit comfortably into a new architectural element in the Japanese home, a tokonoma, or alcove for treasured objects.

A third form of ikebana arose late in the sixteenth century when, the story goes, a samurai paused near a pond for a tea break. Spying an iris growing nearby, he slashed it with his sword and thrust it into his helmet, giving birth to the "thrown-in" style of arrangement known as *nageire*.

This naturalistic, informal style contrasted sharply with the elaborately defined and formal style of *rikka* and the less formal style of the *shoka*. In *nageire*, stems were allowed to cross for the first time in a naturalistic flow. This informality and opportunity for individual expression would, in the course of time and over several centuries, lend itself to a broad audience that included Westerners.

For two-and-a-half centuries (1615–1868), during what is known as the Edo period, Japan was almost entirely cut off from the outside world. With the collapse of the ruling shogunate and the opening of doors to trade in the mid-nineteenth century, the exchange of cultural influences was rapid. Japan quickly assimilated Occidental ways while Europe embraced Japanese art. The asymmetrical and linear lines of woodcuts, for example, translated into the flowing lines of Art Nouveau.

In the realm of flower arranging, these reciprocal influences were important as well. Some in the West found the simpler designs of ikebana appealing and felt that a few flowers placed simply in a container were preferable to the overflowing epergnes of the Victorian era. The Japanese, in turn, were energized by the introduction of exotic cut flowers.

A new school expanded the possibilities even more. In 1926, Sofu Teshigahara—called the Picasso of flower arranging—founded the Sogetsu school. Plant material no longer had to follow natural growth patterns. It could be used as color, form, texture, and line.

If the opening of Japan, beginning in the 1850s and accelerating in the late 1860s, introduced the West to ikebana, the military occupation of Japan following World War II further developed the acquaintance. American and European wives accompanying their husbands had leisure time to explore the arts. They took classes in ikebana in the various

schools and returned home, many doing demonstrations and teaching their new skills. They also entered flower shows with their new ideas, further spreading the form and style of the Japanese art.

Today, the three leading schools of ikebana are Ikenobo, Ohara, and Sogetsu. Ikenobo is the oldest and most classical, its style characterized by restraint and open space. The Ohara school is credited with the introduction of *moribana*, with its low bowl and fuller, naturalistic arrangement, which is popular for Western homes. It was later translated into the triangular open silhouette of the line arrangement. The Sogetsu school is known for its innovative freestyle and abstract designs that may employ masses of plant material. It is this school that has been particularly influential in the development of contemporary European design, such as modern mass. All three schools continue to extend the boundaries of creativity with freestyle designs, as do the more than two thousand other recognized schools of ikebana in Japan. Ikebana today is a vibrant art form, never static, always searching, testing new expressions.

RIKKA

This traditional horizontal *rikka* is made from two junipers cut apart and reassembled with the supplemental material of crab apple, chrysanthemum, azalea, rose of Sharon, and pine. It is staged in front of an installation entitled *The White Cliffs of Dover*, by British artist Cornelia Parker, at the Milwaukee Art Museum.

SHOKA WITH ONE MATERIAL
Maribeth Price

A single variety of flower—iris—is used for the *shin* (tallest/heaven), *soe* (secondary/man), and *tai* (tertiary/earth) in this one-material *shoka* design. This simple, elegant ikebana arrangement rises from a glossy ceramic container that contrasts with the rough stone wall under it. Space, under and above the container, between and under the three floral positions, is as much a component as the flowers themselves. The design carries the eye back to the bridge, the red maple, and the flowering crab apples in the Japanese Garden of the Memphis Botanic Garden, Tennessee.

RIGHT-HANDED TWO-MATERIAL SHOKA
Jane Morgan

Opposite, this two-material *shoka*, called a *nishuike*, is composed of budding peach blossoms and yellow roses. The traditional bronze *usabata* container emphasizes the importance of water and contributes to the classical feeling of the design. The trunklike one-stem placement of the plant material is a *shoka* trademark inherited from the *rikka* form. Elegant restraint and simplicity make this style a popular choice for the Western home. Photograph by Jane Morgan

Expressive Freestyle
Jane Morgan

The sculptural container inspired this expressive freestyle arrangement. Boldly contrasting lilies, carnations, and yellowed hosta leaves, chosen for their end-of-the-season naturalistic quality, create a kaleidoscope of colors and shapes. The delicate bittersweet provides additional interest with line and dot, while repeating shapes and enclosing space. Photograph by Jane Morgan

INTERPRETIVE FREESTYLE
Jane Morgan

In this interpretive freestyle, manipulated papyrus stalks represent sails. "Boots" from a tree dracaena (*Dracaena arborea*) represent wind blowing through the sails; and the croton leaves depict splashing waves. The orange "boots," which repeat the color and shape of the container, are actually the points at which the straplike leaves were attached to the tropical tree. The arranger has not only interpreted a theme but has also called our attention to a seldom noticed form in nature. Photograph by Jane Morgan

Sogetsu Freestyle
Gail Emmons

This freestyle design could complement many a contemporary home or modern art collection. Loops of thin bamboo rise from and return to a black Sogetsu container. A broad strelitzia leaf cuts horizontally across their path, delineating multiple planes even in this narrow design. Three other leaves and red gladioli reinforce the parallel direction while adding strength and color. A line of red bamboo encloses the space on the left to balance the mass on the right.

Ikebana at Home

Arrangement by Dorothy W. Elliott, home of Jane and Bob Pinkas

A centerpiece for a spring buffet—in three low ikebana containers—stretches down the center of a table. The arranger, a teacher in the Ohara school, has gathered material from the early garden—hosta leaves, Solomon's seal, bleeding heart, aquilegia, Japanese primula, scilla, iris, lamb's ears, and azalea—to express "spring" and to harmonize with the colors of the room. A few stems of lilies and peonies—not quite blooming in the garden yet—were purchased and contrast with the finer material.

In the ikebana tradition, the arranger has incorporated space and used asymmetrical balance to create rhythm and interest. The groupings vary in visual weight, in the spacing between them, and in the combinations of material. No two groups contain the same flowers, but each group repeats something in the preceding one, creating a sense of flow and continuity. The directional placement of the stems and leaves "connects" the groups, creating a flowing, unified design. Needle holders support the stems and permit water and space to be important features in the design.

Even though this design is for a buffet table, it has been kept low so as not to compete with the chandelier above. Little or no blue has been used, since blue does not show up well at night.

WHAT THE ARRANGERS SAY

Many arrangers credit ikebana with teaching them to see, to select, and to omit the superfluous. Margaret Hall, an arranger from Shawnee Mission, Kansas, says, "The Sogetsu freestyle was a revelation. I never take a walk anymore that I don't notice the line of a broken branch, the peeling scraps of sycamore bark, unusual seed pods, or even a rusted bit of tailpipe. The day after wind and ice storms I'm out scrounging through the piles of debris on the curb for that 'perfect' branch. I have been known to carry home a car full of tumbleweeds. Ikebana changed the way I design at home and for flower shows."

Mari Tischenko of Orinda, California, says, "My own style leans toward the simple yet bold, with an emphasis on texture and interesting line and movement. I have studied ikebana for many years and feel the discipline—of creating negative space and following the 'less is more' philosophy—is a great influence on my designs. Time and again, in my ikebana classes, our instructor has delighted and amazed us by what she takes out of an arrangement rather than what she adds. In my work I am constantly asking myself what space I am *creating* rather than filling."

DIVIDED *RIKKA*

Jane Morgan

A modern *suiban* holds a two-shin *rikka* design in which the *shin*, or main branch, is divided. Gladioli form the main branches and are supported by chrysanthemum, cleome, safflower blossoms, cattail leaves, and branches of yew. The arrangement, poised on a lacquered base atop an antique spinet, is framed by brass candlesticks and woodcuts of Japanese figures. Photograph by Jane Morgan

LINE-MASS DESIGN
Asta Johnson

This line-mass design shows an early influence of ikebana on Western styles. The open silhouette and limited selection of plant material were adapted for Western homes in the early twentieth century.

In this arrangement, set between two Asian figures in the living room at Filoli, only two kinds of plant material have been used—deep red lilies and conical asparagus fern. This sparseness is in dramatic contrast to the Victorian design on page 13 that employed twenty-one varieties of garden flowers.

The asparagus fern grows naturally in interesting curves and can be further coaxed into desired shapes by tying and leaving to condition in water overnight. Its rough texture contrasts with the glossy surface of the glazed container; green makes the red of the lilies appear even brighter.

WESTERN MASS; EASTERN LINE
Arrangement by Kay Cobb and Susan Harrison,
home of Audrey and Dick Platt

This mantel arrangement, opposite, successfully combines the influences of East and West. The Western love of abundance and bold forms is evident in the lilies at the base. These give way to Apricot Beauty tulips in bud and the delicate white blossoms of flowering cherry, reaching out and incorporating space in the ikebana tradition.

The mirror compounds the illusion of depth in a design that, because of the narrow mantel, has to be one-sided. It is difficult to determine what is real and what is reflected in this seemingly full and well-rounded design.

TABLE TRENDS
Arrangement by Jan Curran and Wayne Willis,
home of Emmy and Billy Winburn

Even in this decidedly Western table centerpiece—featuring a seasonal bunny with pastel ears—the ikebana influence can be seen. Fuller than a traditional ikebana design, the arrangement still suggests the natural growth pattern, and space is part of the design. The budding branches of flowering plum rise above the other springtime offerings of grape hyacinth, scabiosa, sweet William, verbena, and parrot tulips. The whole rests in moss on a silver tray, surrounded by silver chargers, crystal, hurricane globes, and ribboned place cards—ready for the guests to arrive.

To the right and through the doorway, the white blossoms of spathiphyllum can be seen.

Chapter 3 Four Designers and Their Gardens

Opposite: Pink Wave petunias and cerise geraniums, in a planter on Jane Foster's porch, complete the circle begun by the border across the lawn. There for the cutting is a bounty to delight any arranger—pink mallow, white Casa Blanca lily, blue Russian sage, towering globe thistle, sea holly, cosmos, Blue Fascination veronicastram, double filipendula, salvia, nicotiana, bronze fennel, Summer Pink marguerite daisies, snapdragon, monkshood, meadow rue, Buttered Popcorn rose, and more, much more.

All flower arrangers are gardeners. The "garden" may be the grounds and cutting garden of a grand estate, or it may be the philodendron in a city apartment that occasionally contributes a dramatic leaf to an arrangement made with flowers from the corner market. Whatever the size of the "garden," you can't be an arranger without living with plants.

Whether large or small, the garden is such an integral part of flower arranging that, in many cases, it is hard to know which came first, the gardener or the arranger. Did the arranger begin designing with plant material because of the wonders available outside the door? Or did the garden grow out of a desire to have interesting plant material close at hand?

Many a garden in the Northeast, for example, now boasts Harry Lauder's walking stick, curly willow, smokebush, umbrella pine, a large selection of hostas, and a myriad other "cutables" because the arranger-owner wanted a source of interesting branches and foliage close at hand. Similarly, houses and sunrooms have filled up with bromeliads and begonias, succulents and sansevierias, originally purchased for use in a flower arrangement. The plants survived the experience and continue to flourish. Who could throw them out?

In other cases, the garden came first. As the garden grew—as the blossoms of spring turned into the pods and berries and fruits of fall, as the first chartreuse-green leaves matured and then turned gold and crimson—it seemed a shame to the gardener not to bring some of this beauty indoors. A snippet of honeysuckle in a perfume bottle, a branch of Kousa dogwood in the corner of the hallway, a single peony blossom floating in a glass bowl, all were welcomed and enjoyed. Perhaps the next step was to trim the honeysuckle so that the line was clearer; put a few large hosta leaves at the base of the Kousa dogwood for drama, contrast, and balance; add a graceful bit of clematis vine to the peony floating in the bowl.

Just as it is difficult to distinguish between the arranger and the gardener, in a few special instances it is nearly impossible to tell where the garden stops and the home filled with flower arrangements begins. In this section we focus on three arrangers, their gardens, and homes—that are extensions of the lovingly developed gardens that surround them. Then we visit the garden of a designer-sculptor-horticulturist-preservationist to enjoy the color and form and history of the plants he treasures and uses in his large-scale designs.

The first garden belongs to Jane Foster, whose short-season garden in Maine not only surrounds her turn-of-the-twentieth-century cottage but seems to come inside the shingled walls, with garden flowers gracing every nook and cranny, mantel and table. The second gardener-arranger is Pauline Runkle, who began her garden to have wonderful material for the arrangements she does for weddings and festive events. The third is Cecile McCaull, who preserved and restored an early-twentieth-century property and has kept going—creating new gardens, perennial borders, and a walled cutting area for the peach-colored tulips and peonies that she loves to use in her home arrangements. The fourth is Leland Miyano, whose garden in Oahu, Hawaii, is a living museum of plants from around the world, plants that he and other arrangers use in dramatic designs.

JANE FOSTER

On Mount Desert Island, just off the rugged coast of Maine, is Acadia National Park. Forests of hardwood, hemlock, red spruce, white cedar, and balsam fir cover the mountains that rise from the ocean. At sea level, granite ledges sculpted by glaciers embrace coves, and the beaches are paved with surf-smoothed stones called cobbles. Here, the Maine climate is gentled by the ocean to create a short but felicitous growing season.

On the side of a peak near the national park sits Treetops, a summer "cottage" built at the turn of the twentieth century, when summer residents lived the good life on a grand scale with elaborate dinner parties, afternoon teas, and formal dances. (Treetops has eleven bedrooms; its ballroom was torn down during the Great Depression.) The house looks out from the wraparound porch through the tops of towering trees to the Atlantic Ocean, and from the front, sides, and back of the house are other views to delight the visitor. Everywhere in August there are flowers in bloom. Looking toward the sea, one sees a bed of lilies, astilbes, cimicifugas, and hostas. To the right, white hydrangea, burgundy coleus, and sweet potato vine repeat the colors of a paper birch and Japanese maple planted nearby. A rocky area under the trees is carpeted with moss and native bunchberry. A cutting garden offers an armload of five-foot-tall *Astilbe chinensis* var. *taquetti* 'Superba.' In another area Ruby Slipper cardinal flowers are joined by a chorus of red and burgundy plants in what the owner has dubbed the Hotbed of Discontent.

This is the home and garden of Jane Foster. She recalls no early interest in gardening, but here, high above the harbor, there is no doubt that she and the garden have found each other. As you cross the welcoming porch, planters and pots overflow with bloom. The flowers continue when you cross the threshold. More than two dozen arrangements, large and small, casual and more formal, are placed throughout the house—from the kitchen to the dining room, living room, library, and porch. Every blossom is from the garden. "I've arranged flowers all my life, but now I only use flowers from my own garden." Foster says, "I arrange for the Zen-like peace it brings me—and as a tribute to the garden's glorious bounty."

In the flower room–butler's pantry of this 1895 home, the gardener-arranger has cut, conditioned, and placed in containers a selection of herbal specimens. The single stem or handful of blossoms is displayed to advantage whether in a silver stirrup cup or a colored glass bottle.

Hydrangea, blue-black monkshood, delphinium, burgundy coleus, and white physotegia grace three containers on a table set for dinner. Contrast in color and texture is very important, according to the arranger, as well as letting the flowers fall naturally.

The containers, Chinese export, were commissioned by an ancestor and brought home on his clipper ship, the *Courier*. The blue and white of the antique pieces are repeated in the pierced and covered candle-holders.

Vases of white Casa Blanca lilies and warm-colored zinnias line the mantel below a painting of a thirty-pound salmon caught by Foster's father in 1970.

The middle arrangement in the photograph on the previous page takes a place of honor atop a glass table on the porch, opposite. Ammi majus, a cultivated relative of Queen Anne's lace, is surrounded by lavender, mint, and nasturtiums. Jane Foster explains her arranging technique: "I don't think I would know how to arrange commercially grown flowers. How would I know what to do if they didn't tell me, if they didn't curve? They have their own lives and arrange themselves accordingly. I only choose the colors." Chairs, painted by a Mount Desert art teacher, continue the floral theme of the garden and house.

The arbor in the background is covered with Paul's Himalayan musk rose and to the right, on the trellis, is Eden. In the foreground one variety of flower blends with another much as they soon will in arrangements. Hollyhocks promise blossoms a little later, and yellow and white verbascum stand ready to contribute linear forms to an imposing composition.

PAULINE RUNKLE

Pauline Runkle wanted garden roses and hollyhocks, foxgloves and Solomon's seal, to give a natural gardenesque look to the arrangements she did for weddings and the Boston Pops concerts. The only solution was to grow them.

Fifteen years ago, Runkle and her husband, Joe, bought a four-acre site that had been a pig farm. When the house was finished, the garden was begun. Rock ledges were covered with eight trailerloads of loam, then one area after another was planted—a full-sun perennial garden, a shade garden, an antique-rose garden, a meadow garden, and a small orchard of miniature fruit trees. Recently a patch with eight varieties of miniature pumpkins and ten of sunflowers was added.

These gardens certainly offer their own rewards, but they also supply the perfect branch, stem, leaf, or blossom when it is needed for a bride's bouquet or for lavish arrangements at a fund-raiser.

Runkle has had her own design firm since the 1970s. For a number of years, before a budget cut in 1996, her arrangements graced the stage of the Boston Pops for their nationally televised concerts. When the Dalai Lama spoke before a live audience of 12,000 people at Cornell University, her design was in front of the podium.

Her signature style has the look, feel, and fragrance of the garden. In addition to the vanloads of flowers she buys before dawn at the Boston Flower Market, she cuts from her garden. Some things just aren't available in the market very often—hosta leaves, for example; so she grows a wide variety of them, some a foot across. Variegated foliage adds a sparkle to large-mass arrangements, so she has planted variegated Solomon's seal, weigela, and daphne. And in June, when the wedding business is booming, there are roses and more roses— David Austins, vintage roses, and floribundas such as the cherry-apricot Baby Talk. The top performer is Bonica, which refuses to stop blooming in the heat of summer.

Flower arrangements practically make themselves in this garden. Here peach-colored Sally Holmes roses, the lavender blossoms of silver-leafed lamb's ears, and chartreuse lady's-mantle could be instantly bundled together to fill a vase.

In addition to her event work, Pauline Runkle gives demonstrations and offers classes in her barn workroom. A teacher and devotee of yoga, she often begins a flower-arranging workshop with a few minutes of breathing and postures. "Everybody rushes in from doing other things," she explains. "They're in their head, thinking of what they've just done and what they will be doing later. I need them to be in with the flowers. I need them to focus. That's the Zen of flowers."

The focus is definitely on flowers in this garden and home.

Opposite: The pinks, peaches, and yellows of roses, peonies, lilies, stock, and foxgloves are set off by the greens of hydrangeas, lady's-mantle, Solomon's seal, and raspberries in this exuberant arrangement. Blossoms and foliage reach over the lip of the Victorian vase, merging flowers and container into a unified whole.

This celebration of summer illustrates how Pauline Runkle blends market material with foliage and flowers from the garden in her special naturalistic style. From the garden come the arching stems of Solomon's seal, the yellow climbing rose, broad hosta leaves, chartreuse lady's-mantle, columbine, purple malva, branches of raspberry, grasses, and a variety of roses. The other material, out of season in this garden, was purchased in the market—foxgloves, peonies, hydrangeas.

CECILE McCAULL

When Cecile and Phil McCaull bought their 1925 English manor-style house in the mid-1970s, it had been standing empty for five years. The extensive and varied gardens designed by John Greenleaf on the twenty-acre estate were recognizable but sadly neglected. Some treasures, however, could not be missed. One was a towering copper beech and another is the jewel in the property's crown—a hundred-year-old, multitrunked katsura (*Cercidiphyllum japonicum*), the largest in Connecticut and possibly in the world. This specimen "sold" the property to the McCaulls.

Their first task was preservation, then restoration of old-specimen trees and shrubs on the grounds—weeping beeches, katsuras, lindens, lace-leaf maples, lace-bark maples, and tulip magnolias. Phil McCaull takes on the arboreal responsibilities, including the maintenance of a line of mature, pleached linden that are pruned three times a season. The blight that hit New England dogwoods in the 1970s exerted its toll on this Connecticut property, and the McCaulls were forced to replace eighty-five dogwood trees in 1979.

Cecile, a Memphis native, took to the New England soil and climate with determination, enrolling in courses on gardening and landscape design at the Garden Education Center in Greenwich and at the New York Botanical Garden. Knowledge gained was assimilated, put into practice, and then enriched with weeklong courses on landscape design in Charleston, South Carolina, and on plants and trees at Williams College, Williamstown, Massachusetts, with horticulture gurus Michael Dirr and Allen Armitage.

Study and travel have trained her eye, deepened her understanding, and fueled her enthusiasm. Every trip or seminar, she says, inspires a new garden. One such product is a walled garden in the Charleston style, which keeps the deer away from peach-colored tulips in the spring and vegetables and delphiniums in the summer. Another garden inspired by a seminar features more than a hundred yards of perennial borders. They line a grassy path that leads to a pond at the lower end of the twenty-acre estate. A wildflower garden has been started behind the borders.

Cecile McCaull is definitely a gardener, but she is also a flower arranger, as anyone who enters her home will quickly see. She has studied with the English arranger and teacher Sheila Macqueen, whose clear message is that arrangements should come from and reflect the garden. They certainly do in the McCaull home, where the yellows and apricots of the decor are brought to life with the flowers and foliage from the garden. It would be hard to say which was the finer work by this artist—the garden or the beautiful flower-filled home.

In the entrance hall, two urns purchased in Bath, England, hold armloads of garden flowers— Coral Charm and Duchesse de Nemours peonies, Montrachet lilies, Leonidas and Femma roses, white stock, hydrangeas, phlox, and purple brodiaeas.

Square planters with delicate fairy roses, geraniums, and violas line the pool terrace. Bolder accents—burgundy elephant's-ear and chartreuse sweet potato vine, coleus, and daisy—tumble from other pots. In the distance, inspired by the White Garden at Sissinghurst, the first white of the all-white border is just coming into bloom.

Opposite: A Herend bowl is flanked by two footed containers, extending the warm colors of the flowers the full length of this table set for dinner. The three containers hold combinations of peach lilies, Leonidas roses, chartreuse lady's-mantle, white phlox, and Dutch hydrangea. China and linens in the same pattern and coral candles in the background leave no doubt as to this hostess's favorite color.

A classic container that mimics the color and shape of the boats in the painting by Bernard Gantner holds green-and-white hosta leaves, green hydrangea, fern, lady's-mantle, and the almost-black burgundy of copper beech and euphorbia. Famed teacher Sheila Macqueen would surely approve of this subtle all-foliage arrangement from the garden, which reflects the light and shadow of the painting, without disrupting the stillness of low tide.

LELAND MIYANO

Twenty years ago Leland Miyano purchased a one-acre building plot on the Hawaiian island of Oahu. It had been scraped clean of rocks, bulldozed flat, and planted in an acre of lawn. Today it is a fantasy garden, a tropical wonderland of plants from around the world. Almost every greenhouse plant you've ever seen—ferns, philodendrons, bromeliads, dracaena, and many you could not have imagined—are flourishing here. Paths meander through dense growth with something to amaze the eye at every turn and every level. Towering Macarthur palms (*Ptychosperma macarthurii*), native to New Guinea, host a giant staghorn fern (*Platycerium superbum*) with six-foot-long "antlers." The bamboolike stem of the sealing wax palm (*Cyrtostachys renda*) is as red as the wax it is named after. Orchids grow from succulents that cling to trees. There are bromeliads with speckled foliage and lilies with striped leaves. The huge *hookeri* is just one of the anthurium varieties growing in this flower arranger's paradise.

Miyano offers cutting privileges to his fellow garden club members and uses the plants in his own design work. He is a sculptor, landscape designer, and creator of displays—very large arrangements of plant material and stone. His exotic creative installations have welcomed guests to many major events in Hawaii, including fund-raising galas at the Museum of Contemporary Art.

Miyano began work on his garden slowly, planting a small area at a time, the better to observe how things grew. He brought in boulders for natural accents, moving each one, he said, at least twice. Many of the plants were collected during the fifteen years Miyano worked and traveled with his friend and mentor Roberto Burle Marx, the Brazilian artist and landscape architect. Often the two would arrive at sites being cleared by bulldozers, snatching orchids and bromeliads from fallen trees. Some of these rescues were donated to botanical gardens and others flourish in the haven Miyano has created.

Not all the plants in the Miyano garden are rare, but all are interesting. There's not a dull one in the lot. "I'm interested in all tropical plants," he said, "but I had to do a lot of traveling before I realized how unique the Hawaiian flora is. Seeing the damage to the rain forest in Brazil made me realize the fragility of the environment. Now I'd like to grow only Hawaiian endemics, but many are already extinct."

Most of the plants in Miyano's garden have been grown from seed, spores, or cuttings, and many represent species now extinct elsewhere in the world. The garden is a constantly changing scene, depending on what grows, what works, and what doesn't. "One thing about my garden," he explains, "I am not afraid to put plants in and I am not afraid to take plants out." He sees the garden as his experiment, his personal classroom. "The plants tell me what to do," he says. "My garden is the story of my relationship with nature."

Bromeliads, cycads, and the feathery *Pilea serpyllacea* hug a rock that Miyano carried onto his once-barren plot. A ti plant (*Cordyline terminalis*), much loved by arrangers, sparkles red and gold in the background.

The spider lily (*Crinum asiaticum*) is even more popular for its seedpods than for its bloom.

Opposite: This *Aechmea polyantha* was discovered in Amazonia in 1973 and recorded by the British botanical artist Margaret Mee. It has not been found since. In 1984, Mee gave Miyano eight seeds; three were viable. The two surviving plants have been growing in Miyano's garden for seventeen years, and one was blooming for the first time in April 2001. A few of its tiny blossoms opened each morning and, natural pollinators being absent, Miyano transferred the pollen from one blossom to the next with a bit of fern, hoping for seeds that will preserve its future.

Anthuriums come in many shapes and sizes, including these two marvels in Miyano's garden. The leaves of *Anthurium hookeri* are green, glossy, and up to three feet long, dramatic in arrangements. The "pigtail" anthurium, opposite, is *Anthurium scherzeranum x wendlingeri*.

The Honolulu Academy of Art is the perfect setting for large-scale material from Miyano's garden. Here a stalk of *Heliconia vellerigera* rises from a heavy, glazed container. It is complemented in texture and scale by wrappings of leaves from the lily *Crinum* species 'Kaaawa' and a cluster of bulblets from another lily, *Crinum infructescence*.

The heliconia is from the Ecuadorian Amazon. The deep red bracts hold the true, or day, flowers; a yellow one can be seen peeking from an upper bract. The tactile quality of the bracts has been compared to soft kitten fur. When the artist and landscape designer Roberto Burle Marx saw the blossoms in Miyano's garden, he said, "A monkey has made love to this plant!"

On the plant, the bracts hold their appearance for six months or more. Photograph by Linny Morris Cunningham

The size of this blossom, opposite, can be gauged by the forms at the bottom—coconuts still in their husks. This is the inflorescence of the traveler's palm (*Ravenala madagascariensis*), which can weigh forty pounds or more and exceed four feet in height and three feet in width. The host plant is not really a palm but rather is related to *Heliconia* and *Strelitzia*. "Travelers to Madagascar where this plant is native," Miyano says, "reputedly drank from the leafbases, which hold water. My experience is that this water would be used only in dire emergencies as the smell is putrid and it is stained with undesirables." Photograph by Linny Morris Cunningham

SECTION TWO

Flower Shows—
The Arranger's Arena

Every artist seeks an audience for his work—the painter, the architect, the filmmaker, the musician, the ballet dancer. Flower arrangers find this audience in a flower show. But there's an added dimension—competition. The flower show is not only the gallery and stage, it is also the arena, the tennis court, the chess board, the bridge table, the golf course for this challenging sport.

Some people say they love to arrange flowers for the home but would never enter a show, yet many others respond to the stimulus of competition, knowing that their concentration will be more acute, their effort more focused, their creativity more inspired than if they had not tackled a flower show entry. Does a tennis player concentrate harder, play better if he or she is just rallying with a friend, hitting the ball back and forth over the net, or is in a real game? Flower shows, for arrangers, are the real game.

Defined Space. See page 80.

Flower shows and their accompanying competition are not new. Records of the Pennsylvania Horticultural Society, the oldest such organization in the United States, refer to a flower show (public exhibition) in 1829. By 1842 the flower show tradition was well established, and the minutes refer to "The 14th Annual Exhibition of the Pennsylvania Horticultural Society." The Committee on Flowers awarded a "best" and "next best" for designs of a triumphal arch, a grotto, an urn composed of flowers, a pair of festoons, and a bouquet.

One of the entries in "floral designs, festoons, and bouquets" was a twenty-foot-high triumphal arch by Samuel Maupay, described as "a light and neat structure in proper proportion and embellished with taste." A gardener named Joseph Cook created a ten-foot-tall grotto, "encased in all its parts with flowers," which covered an area of fifteen feet. The minutes applauded the effort; "In this design which was entirely original the contributor has shown much ingenuity and taste; the architectural form of the grotto was unique and commanded the attention and admiration of every visitor."

These huge constructions are precursors of the large-scale designs, such as the room class, now featured in the Philadelphia Flower Show. This event, sponsored each March by the Pennsylvania Horticultural Society, draws an attendance of 285,000 visitors.

While most of the early arrangers were men, in 1862, in order to encourage more participation from women, the Pennsylvania Horticultural Society announced the introduction of a "beautiful Silver Medal . . . as a special premium to Lady Competitors."

About the same time, in 1861, the Royal Horticultural Society of England held its first flower-arrangement competition. According to Dorothy Cooke and Pamela McNicol in their book *A History of Flower Arranging* (1989), the first competitive class called for "the decoration of a dinner table. . . . Baskets of any materials, china vases, glass dishes or epergnes" could be used. The winning entry was created by T. C. March, although it was understood his sisters actually did the arrangement. The table decoration consisted of three tall stands, each with three tiers of delicate plant material—maiden hair and other ferns, forget-me-nots, lilies of the valley, pansies, rosebuds, and small bunches of grapes. Each stand was composed of "a glass dish as a base with a slender glass stem from twelve to fifteen inches in length, on top of which rests a smaller glass dish and from the centre of this a cornucopia or trumpet-shaped vase."

His design could still grace a buffet or banquet table, and that day in June of 1861 it created a sensation. In her book *Flora Domestica: A History of British Flower Arranging, 1500–1930* (published in 2000), Mary Rose Blacker quoted a letter from an unnamed girl that was published in *The Gardener's Chronicle*:

"I forget the 2nd and 3rd prizes, indeed in the crush I am afraid I was pushed past without seeing them, but the moment my eye rested on one group, I said, 'Oh, there is the best of all' and was lost in admiration of the exquisite arrangement of the three pieces. I was delighted to see on the card at the foot, 1st Prize, for it was my idea of the perfection of refined taste."

The second and third prizes, drawings of which appear in Blacker's book, show the traditional style of the day—heavy mounds of pineapple and grapes with brightly colored begonia leaves, some orchids and palm fronds—designs *The Chronicle* described as "lumpish."

T. C. March, who was not a professional plants person but worked in Lord Chamberlin's office, is credited with revolutionizing table decoration. Within a month, a firm in London was selling March Stands. The fashionable Victorian home relied on these devises for the next two or three decades.

Soon after his flower show triumph, in 1862, March published *Fruit and Flower Decoration*, a book that gave detailed instructions on how to support flowers in the shallow saucers that constituted levels of his stand, a device used until the development of the present-day Oasis. Blacker quotes from March's book: "Flowers have hitherto been arranged almost exclusively in tall vessels filled with water only, but it is different with wide shallow vessels where damp sand and clay must be used . . . then you have the power of planting each flower-stalk and leaf by itself in the exact position and at the precise height you choose." He recommended concealing the sand and clay with moss or fern leaves.

March also gave advice on dominance and unity in the artistic design of the arrangement, saying, "it will not suffice to crowd in a quantity of different flowers with no relationship to each other . . . for people who have correct and refined taste it will be necessary to adopt some definite design or leading idea, which must be adhered to more or less throughout the arrangement." March took inspiration from the bouquets sold in Paris markets that featured one or two colors of plant material arranged in bands.

This case—of a prizewinning entry almost a century and a half ago—illustrates both the purpose and influence of flower shows. Flower shows large and small summon fresh designs and innovative mechanics and present them on a stage for public viewing. People come, drawn by the indefinable power of flowers. Once there, visitors are captured, as the young writer at the first competition was, by the elegance and originality of the arrangements. They go away with ideas and inspiration for their own floral artistry; ideas that are shared with family and friends. New fashions take hold and move not just around the town, but around the world. Mr. March took an idea from the streets of Paris, made it his own, and gave it to the flower-arranging world—an idea that still has merit. In *Flora Domestica*, Blacker showed how to make a modern-day March Stand—using cake tins and a metal tray.

In the following pages we feature arrangements created in response to a flower show schedule and the class requirements, just as March's design adhered to the specification "decoration for a dinner table." These designers interpret the class title, respect the space allotment, and in some cases create in a particular style. We begin in Chapter 4 with tables and how arrangers use this familiar form, as T. C. March did, as staging for new design styles and techniques. In the next chapter, "Space—Defined and Contained," we see how a specific background or an enclosed niche does not limit creativity but instead concentrates it. And in Chapter 6, "Pedestals—Elevated Elegance," designs are placed on pedestals as the works of art they indeed are.

With a nod to that other art, fashion design, we see designer gowns complemented by equally elegant arrangements, hats that could have stepped out of a Parisian millinery shop, and jewelry that we wish was real—all in Chapter 7, "Floral Fashions—Botanic Couture."

The art of flower arranging then moves into the art museum where it interprets and enhances works of fine art, as discussed in Chapter 8. We close this section with Chapter 9 by taking flower arrangement out of doors and into complementary settings that can add an extra dimension, allowing for an interplay between a floral work of art and its surroundings. An arrangement called "Singin' in the Rain," for example, takes on an added sparkle in the mist of a fountain. The architectural quality of an abstract design is accentuated by the lines of a building.

It is a journey of discovery. An open eye and an open mind will be rewarded with the excitement of this new art and the potential for new ideas. Every arrangement is not to everyone's liking, but neither is every piece of art in a museum. Every arrangement is the expression of its artist-arranger.

To see this art form as the arranger sees it one must look at flowers, foliage, stems, bark, and branches in a new light. These natural forms become the medium—the painter's oils, the sculptor's stone, the architect's bricks. The master Belgian flower arranger Daniel Ost wrote in *Leafing Through Flowers* (2000), "When a flower is cut and thus deprived of both its source of nutrition and its future . . . it undergoes a change that must be understood as the entry into a new and extremely intense sequence of life. Whether the flower is alone—appearing only with others of its species in repetition—or grouped in a scene with many different actors, it inevitably takes on another meaning because the way we look at it has changed, too."

Consciously or unconsciously, the plant material is transformed from flower, fruit, foliage, stem, branch, and bark into color, form, line, texture, pattern, and space. These elements of design are found in all the arts and are the basic qualities to which we have responded since ancient times. The vibrant color of a lily, the molded form of a calla, the sweeping line of a wisteria vine, the rough texture of bark, the pattern of a maple leaf, the space in and around a tulip—all are the brush and palette of flower arranging. The designer selects and arranges these elements according to the principles of design—balance, rhythm, dominance, contrast, scale, and proportion. The viewer might look at the arrangement and ask, as the judges do:

Art on a Pedestal. See page 90.

- **Balance** Is there visual stability throughout the design? Does it look as though it might topple? Is it bottom heavy?
- **Rhythm** Does the eye move through the design? Or is it stopped by a "bull's-eye"?
- **Dominance** Is one element—line, color—clearly dominant, or is the design confused by several weaker elements?
- **Contrast** Is there a contrasting element, such as texture, to create interest and accentuate the dominant one?
- **Scale** Is the size relationship of the components pleasing, or does the large flower seem out of scale for the tiny container?
- **Proportion** Is one area of the design (the plant material, for example) in good relationship to the other areas (the container, for example)? Or does the amount of plant material seem skimpy for the large container?

These elements and principles combine to create a unified design, a work of art all the more precious because it uses the unforgivably ephemeral medium of fresh flowers. As one arranger said, "You have to come around, somehow, to putting enough value in the beauty of the moment to feel it's a worthwhile endeavor." On the following pages the beauty of the moment has been captured, and the arrangers share with the reader their inspiration and interpretation. They hope the viewer will see what they see.

Chapter 4   Tables—A Feast for the Eyes

Tables are among the most popular classes in a flower show—both for the arrangers and for the viewers. Arrangers like tables because they are familiar, a friendly form from the home, used for everything from cereal boxes and milk cartons to precious porcelain and silver candelabra. Tables are, simply, less intimidating, more approachable than pedestals and niches. Even a novice arranger can visualize the components needed—breakfast dishes or dinnerware, tablecloth or place mats, container, flowers, napkins.

This feeling of familiarity holds true for the viewer as well as the arranger. First-time flower show visitors might feel a little lost in front of abstract compositions on pedestals and synergistic designs in niches, but tables they appreciate. There might even be an idea to take home.

This familiarity of staging, however, in no way limits the creativity that can be expressed. A table class offers a challenge and an opportunity to the most experienced arranger.

In flower shows there are two types of table classes—functional and exhibition. A functional table, as the term suggests, is set for food service. An exhibition table moves away from the service of food to artistic composition, with only a suggestion of food or drink. The table becomes, in effect, a still life.

"CEÇI N'EST PAS UNE TABLE," an homage to Magritte
Gay Estes

"To communicate, with the fewest possible components, the idea of a surreal meal" was this designer's goal. The title is a reference to René Magritte's painting of a pipe, at the bottom of which he states, in French, "This is not a pipe."

The tablecloth, made of artist's canvas, the wine bottle, plate, and glass were all painted by the arranger, recalling the trompe l'oeil of Magritte's stone tables. The sweeping rhythm of the container—a candlestick by metal artist Bill Peck, twisted in the firing—is continued in the painted wine glass and in the massed-line arrangement of amaranthuses, lilies, roses, heliconias, pears, and assorted pods, seeds, and berries. The palette moves from the dull umber of the metal and stone to the warm tones of the flame atop the bottle—fashioned from Fimo modeling clay and reminiscent of the fire images in Magritte's work. Is this a Magritte joke—firewater?

The abundance of fruit, flowers, and foliage held aloft is in ironic contrast to the desolate landscape below. The stone table offers only a green apple, the artist's signature. There's a rich feast here, but for the eyes alone.

SUPPER IN THE BOUDOIR OF A VENETIAN COURTESAN
*Ainslie Todd and
Beth Buchignani*

A painting by Caroline Russell depicting arches reminiscent of those of Piazza San Marco sets the scene, opposite. An eighteenth-century Venetian side chair, a set of nineteen-century Venetian wine goblets, a gilt stool in the Savonarola style, and lengths of Fortuny fabrics, all borrowed from friends and family, lead the viewer into the fantasy. A velvet-covered board across a French copper bathtub holds a silver tray set for supper, to be shared perhaps by the bathing courtesan and her admirer seated in the chair.

An antique figure supports an extravagant bouquet of tulips, lilies, roses, hydrangeas, delphiniums, and bells of Ireland, furthering the sense of luxury and elegance in this Renaissance still life. The long-stemmed French tulips seem to have a mind of their own, much like the Venetian courtesan who inspired this arrangement.

THE ARTIST'S TABLE—ADOLPH GOTTLIEB
Irene Davis

The flower show schedule asked this designer to create a table "arranged artistically to give only the suggestion of dining" and inspired by a painter, musician, sculptor, potter, dancer, or other artist.

As docent at an exhibition of Adolph Gottlieb's grid paintings, this arranger had become familiar with his imagery—personal and universal objects held in tension on a flat plane. Her flat plane is a tablecloth stitched with a black-ribbon grid. Early modern, square china belonging to her parents is all that suggests the dining and ties the artist to the 1940s, when he lived in Brooklyn.

The grid theme is continued in the sculptural container, fashioned to the arranger's specifications by a metalworker, which adds height to the overall design. The grid pattern is repeated again in the arrangement with two lines of bent equisetum. Orange lilies and cream-colored rice flowers echo the colors of the china and contrast with the seeded eucalyptus and leucadendron. An orange-and-cream napkin with a subtle grid pattern completes the picture. The whole is photographed in front of another grid—a wall of windows centered by a fireplace.

BREAKFAST AT THE SPIRIT HOUSE OF PENANG
Sophie Coors and Suzanne Mallory

You are invited to breakfast at dawn in the singular quiet of this spirit house on the island of Penang. What nectar awaits in the silk-ribboned goblets? Lift the begonia leaf on the oriental grapefruit and consider making this fantasy journey a real one. Here you can wander through the rain forest, hear the birds and frogs, and follow the wind to a spirit house—a primitive structure built for meditation and prayer. Flowers and notes left as offerings to the spirits of departed loved ones invite you to pause.

   This spirit house is framed in branches of crape myrtle, centered by a tower of wood and bark dripping with string-of-beads (*Senecio rowleyanus*). The flower offering is a fantasy composed of the fruit of monstera encircled by equisetum, supporting burgundy calla lilies and an orchid—*Paphiopedilum* 'Saint Swithin.'

TIME FOR TEMPTATION
Susan Grau and Geri Forrester

A blue trout rises to temptation. The "trout stream," glistening with green, yellow, and brown glass marbles, is made of fabricated Plexiglas set atop a mirror. In it, a swiftly flowing current of New Zealand flax moves past moss-covered "rocks" of Oasis, mounded with cascades of callas, fungi, scented geranium leaves, hostas, hellebores, heuchera leaves, and Flutterby roses.

This symbolic stream flows down the center of a lavish picnic table on which multiple layers of translucent place mats, plates, bowls, and goblets repeat the watery texture and the gold, green, and blue of the stream.

COCKTAILS WITH I. M. PEI
Ann Kobs and Grace Friend

How to suggest the renowned architect, I. M. Pei on a table set for cocktails? This team took their lead from Pei's *Pyramide* at the Louvre in Paris, which is held together by bowstring-tensioning, similar to the technology used in fine sailing boats. This nautical connection is interpreted with leaves from houseplants—dracaena, spathiphyllum, sansevieria—which form a triangle, backed by bamboo and cabling in the shape of sails and spinnakers. A massing of red carnations contrasts with the green foliage.

An erecting company fashioned the pyramid of heavy-duty cable, but it was turned upside down and topped with a round of glass by the arrangers. The jet-black Japanese container repeats the triangular shape, as do the festive cocktail glasses. The arrangers telephoned Mr. Pei, who responded with a video of his work and a warm wish for success. The video is visible on the table, under a pair of horn-rimmed glasses in the style the architect wears.

WEALTH IN THE WETLANDS
Janet Baker, Susan Bodin, and Ann Waldman

The motivation for this table came from the beautiful Oregon wetlands and a nugget of information in a government publication—that there is the potential for growing more biomass per square acre in the wetlands than in the tropical rain forest. How to pay homage to this richness while dining alfresco was the challenge. A unique expression was called for and inspiration was found in the works of two artists renowned for their creations with natural materials—the English sculptor Andy Goldsworthy and the Belgian floral designer Daniel Ost.

Moisture-loving curly willow—eight to ten feet long—is bundled to form the pedestal for this table. The tops of the bundle are bent at table height and woven around, across, and in between each other, depending on the natural direction of the tendrils. Extra pieces add support and help create a symmetrical flat surface. Willow, the arrangers learned, is most amenable to this treatment in spring when it is pliable and waxy.

Continuing the natural theme of their design, the arrangers formed the dinnerware and "vases" from clay and fired them unglazed so they would resemble eggshells in texture and form. Chargers, plates, and bowls, interspersed with leaves and fern fronds and topped with apples, continue the layering begun with the willow. Goblets of pitcher plant tucked into the woven willow add height.

The lushness of the wetlands is reflected in the large number of components, but the colors and textures are carefully limited, resulting in a harmonious, unified whole that intrigues with its originality and complexity.

THE SKY'S THE LIMIT
Ann S. Mastrangelo and Ginnie Tietjens

When is a table class more than a table? At the Philadelphia Flower Show exhibitors are given space to create a whole scene; the table is just one component. The class title of the entry pictured here was "The Sky's the Limit," with exhibitors instructed to give a suggestion of alfresco dining.

A travel article led these exhibitors to focus on the sky over White Sands National Monument in New Mexico. Nocturnal visitors, they learned, are welcomed once a month—on the occasion of the full moon—to party, surf the dunes, or just gaze at the moonlight on the rhythmic patterns in the sand. What a perfect setting for a little alfresco dining.

Two pieces of cypress, bought years earlier, serve as a bench and the

table—in the foreground and atop the dune. A depression in the table serves as a container for the required arrangement. The dune in this design is a plywood form covered with unbleached muslin, sprayed with watered-down white paint and sprinkled with sand. As the muslin dried, it shrunk and the sand adhered to create a dunelike quality. Eight hundred pounds of tropical play sand surrounds the dune. Fingertips drawn across the surface of the sand mimic the patterns of the relentless winds. Cacti identify the arid setting, while four-foot-high swirls of ting ting tell of the desert winds. With a nod to another New Mexico treasure, Georgia O'Keeffe, calla lilies repeat the stark white of the gymsum, and the rhythmic curves of antlers offer contrast to the horizontal and vertical lines. A Minimalist repast of wine and bosc pears awaits the diner.

Chapter 5 Space—Defined and Contained

Space is an element of design, one of the ingredients the arranger has to work with along with form, texture, pattern, line, and size. Space, we propose, may be the most important element, the primary determining factor of a design. The arranger's first question is, Where will the arrangement be placed—what is the space, the framework, it will occupy? Is the arrangement going to be the focal point of a museum lobby or is it going to sit in the narrow hallway of an early American home? Space influences the other elements, especially size—the overall scale of the arrangement as well as the size of the components—and strongly affects proportion.

In flower shows, the schedule indicates the space that an arranger will have to work with. In the first three designs in this chapter the space is indicated by the colored backgrounds—yellow, purple, and blue; these become the canvas on which the arranger paints a picture. The space for the remaining designs is defined by the walls of the niches.

The challenge in both settings is to fill the space without overfilling it. Just as an overly voluptuous arrangement in a narrow hallway feels crowded, so does a design that threatens to exceed its boundaries, whether against a background or in a niche. A useful formula is to leave one-twelfth of the space around the border free. Think of it as imaginary matting framing the picture. Size of the components matters, too. Our eye is accustomed to plant materials being at least one-and-a-half times as tall as the container. A vase that is half the height of the niche will be difficult to fill with a pleasing amount of flowers.

These defined spaces are challenging in another way, too. Because attention is drawn into a smaller, more confined area than, say, the tabletops in the preceding chapter, the viewer is likely to focus more closely and notice more. Colors, shapes, textures, and especially scale and proportion take on added significance.

COLORS THAT COMPLEMENT
Molly B. Stephan

Purple allium and liatris stand in bold contrast to the bright yellow of this background. The geometric forms— lines and spheres—are strong enough to visually fill the space, even though they are concentrated in the center. The color of the background is as much a part of this picture as the plant material and container.
A few yellow chrysanthemums, resting on the black grid that serves as the container, bring the background color into the design, while a purple underlay accentuates the contrast and unifies the design.

COLORS THAT COMPLEMENT

Margaret Weatherly Hall

Painted with cadmium red acrylic, the bamboo stakes in this arrangement, opposite, offer a direct complement to the blue-green of the background. The irregular heights avoid monotony and create a rhythmic pattern against the contrasting background. Red-orange lilies at the base of the design link the parallel lines.

COLORS THAT COMPLEMENT

Carole R. Read

Dried seed heads of *Allium christophii* from the arranger's garden explode with energy, the three bursting forth from the source of all energy—the sun, here crafted from a reed mat and glued to a base.

Depth is achieved by the globular shapes and by the subtle front-to-back placement of the allium stalks in the reed mat. The airy seed heads fill the space without crowding it. All components are painted yellow, the direct complement of the violet of the background.

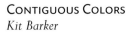

CONTIGUOUS COLORS
Kit Barker

A lush offering of waxy bromeliad blossoms in yellows and corals—
Aechmea, Neoregelia, Guzmania, Vriesea—fairly glows, contrasting with the
brown lines of costus sticks, the curves of dracaena, and the dark green
horizontal container.

The walls of the niche, painted soft peach to harmonize with the
plant material, frame the design. The fabric-covered base continues the
color theme while offering a contrast of texture.

CONTRASTS IN COLORS
Lucy Belding

The sides, back, and floor of this niche are painted yellow, all the better
to highlight the dark forms that float in midair. Clematis twigs sprayed
black and salt cedar twigs painted glossy red hold red and green anthurium
and multicolored croton. The yellow of the background makes a subtle
appearance in the pistil of the anthurium and the veining of the croton.

"LOVELY HULA HANDS"
Heidi Ho Conjugacion and Joyce Tomonari

This niche design, opposite, in a flower show in Hawaii interprets the
lines of the classic island song "Lovely hula hands . . . graceful as the birds
in motion."

Here, *ipu*, the percussive gourds used by hula dancers, serve as
containers for clusters of homegrown heliconia. The three containers
are tied together by threads of black coral and 'Ohi'a tree roots,
reminiscent of the rolls of the ocean current. The "lovely hula hands"
of heliconia point to "birds in motion"—stems of another heliconia, red-
orange psittacorum. The whole forms a synergistic arrangement—one in
which multiple containers are used to create a unified design.

FILLING A NICHE—HOW DO THEY DO THAT?

A niche offers challenges and opportunities for any arranger, whether filling a corner at home or creating a design for a recessed opening at a flower show. At the Philadelphia Flower Show, niches come in all sizes—small, medium, and large—and filling a niche has been honed to an art form.

Exhibitors receive a scale drawing of their niche and a description of the lighting available. Repeat arrangers at the Philadelphia Flower Show—and there are many—often use colored lights, spots, or fireproof gels, and some arrangers even drop fireproof plugs behind false backs to bring a beam of light up from the bottom or in from the side.

A repeat arranger is likely to have a basement, garage or workroom set up with exact replicas of the niches at the show. Over the long winter months a mock-up of a proposed design will be placed in the proper-size niche and altered dozens of times. Fabrics and elegant paper will be installed on the back, sides and floor of the niche. Mat board may be cut to partially cover the opening and frame the floral design that will eventually go inside. Ingenious mechanics, designed to magically suspend plant material and other components, will be devised.

The results intrigue show visitors, who line up to wend their way past the entries, choosing their own favorites and trying to unravel the mystery of the creations—how did they do that?

PACIFIC RIM
Gretchen Riley

With the elegance and mystery of a geisha, a dendrobium emerges from between layers of shoji screen. The class title, "Pacific Rim," and this orchid blooming in the arranger's greenhouse inspired the design. The flower is complemented by the clean lines and simplicity of the miniature shoji screens, built from tiny pieces of balsa wood and rice paper. Subtle lighting contributes to the mystery of the scene.

OUT OF AFRICA
Hope Fox Coates and Hope Coates Eberle

An amber light illuminates a manzanita root that grows out of a diamond-shaped opening, angled to increase the sense of depth and to suggest the mystery of the title, "Out of Africa." The matte board covering has the look of animal skin, and its velvety surface is repeated in the texture of the pink mink protea. A shiny split-leaf philodendron leaf offers contrast.

All components were chosen to communicate the African theme—the shape of the opening recalls diamond mining; the protea and philodendron flourish on the Southern tip of the continent; and the manzanita's shape is reminiscent of solitary trees growing on the African savanna.

"Repeat arrangers" is hardly an adequate term to describe this mother-daughter team. This entry marked the senior member's forty-first year of participating in the Philadelphia Flower Show and her daughter's fourteenth.

HOOKED ON TIME
Gabrielle S. Haab

Following the ikebana mantra that less is more, this arranger limits her components to three lilies embraced by three hooks—one with clock hands in a nod to the class title, "Hooked on Time." Polished stones unite the components and conceal the opening through which the hooks are anchored underneath. The curved background repeats the curve of the hooks, its color echoing the warm tone of the flowers.

HOOKED ON TIME
Marty Van Allen

The gold background glows in the soft lighting of this medium niche, setting off a clock face that appears suspended in space. It is in fact screwed to wooden pegs and held aloft by a weighted lamp base, all concealed by the background. A hook holds a brass pendulum that appears to swing to and fro with tiny callas pointed in opposite directions. Boxwood conceals a bit of Oasis and adds the contrast of texture and color. Double matting, cut by a framer, repeats the shape and colors of the clock face and sets off the composition like a treasured print.

WATCHING THE CLOCK
Patricia A. S. Carson

The opening of this niche, opposite, recalls the shape of a French travel clock. Inside the frame, gears, diminishing in size, appear ready to rotate and recede into the background. This illusion of depth and suspension is aided by two pieces of Lucite and a curving path that starts at the bottom right with the upward-facing orchid, then moves up to the left and back to the right, ending above the orchid.

Chapter 6   Pedestals–Elevated Elegance

T he most popular staging for flower shows is a pedestal—and for good reason. A pedestal elevates the flower arrangement to eye level, sets it apart from it surroundings, and gives it prominence—much like a piece of sculpture placed on a pedestal in a museum or gallery, or in the home. In some homes, a pedestal serves as the designated place for a flower arrangement, much as the tokonoma in the Japanese home holds an ikebana design.

The principle of filling a space but not crowding it applies to pedestal arrangements as it does to the table designs in Chapter 4 and the compositions against backgrounds and in niches in Chapter 5. The dimensions of the space may not be so clearly drawn as in the previously discussed staging, but they are implied by the size and shape of the pedestal, the background, and even by the height of the ceiling. A slim Lucite cube, a robust Ionic column, a stack of apple crates, can all serve as pedestals, but each suggests a different treatment. The pedestal becomes part of the design.

VEGETABLES IN MOTION
Julie Lapham

The chartreuse green of fava beans, hot and sweet peppers, and broccoflower lead the eye through this sculptural vegetable arrangement. A basket of dried jungle vine, integrated into the design, holds the other components and initiates the rhythmic movement of the arrangement. Curves of the vine and loops of ti leaves enclose space and offer contrast to the weightiness of the vegetables, as does the leucadendron and clipped sago palm. Vegetables and leaves are wedged into a core of Oasis, achieving a delicate balance that belies the actual weight of the components.

Vegetable Views
Lou Greer

Two ikebana containers are the spine of this multilevel design, opposite, which intrigues with its contrasting plant material and recessed openings. The tall upper container is actually a long horizontal with an off-center opening. Turned on end and taped to the lower square vase, it holds a little water in the end to keep the asparagus fresh. The bok choy is also in water. (Most vegetables, the arranger found, react to conditioning in the same way as flowers.)

A cage of Oasis taped to the top holds parrot tulips and pittosporum, as well as artichokes, green beans, and radishes secured with bamboo skewers. White pearl onions peek from the opening at the bottom, contrasting with the black container and completing the green-and-white design. A dark palette—eggplant, beets, and burgundy parrot tulips—would create a very different but equally beautiful design.

Botanical Art
Maryjo Garre

Showcasing just one vegetable—the artichoke—in two stages of its growth is the focus of this design, which is reminiscent of a framed botanical print. (The "frame" is a bi-level votive candleholder.) Green cymbidium orchids lead the eye upward, repeat the color of the artichoke, and offer textural contrast.

LUXURIANT LEVELS
Melinda Earle

A rain-forest canopy and its understory inspired this two-part design, opposite. Red dogwood branches spring from a base of floral foam and support more branches woven into an airy but sturdy structure. Plant material chosen for its ability to last out of water—ming fern and leucadendron—adds life to the top, while roots of a giant fig tree and more ming fern lead the eye to the base. Here, a pavé of lichen, moss, and split mahogany pods forms a background for white protea and the architectural forms of bent equisetum.

A BRIGHT NEW MILLENNIUM
Catherine Beattie

A modernistic sculpture sets the tone of this crisp, abstract design, suggesting bright possibilities for the new millennium. The rotating stems and blossoms of green anthurium create rhythm, while red peppers offer color contrast and bring the eye back into the center. Galax leaves, concealing the container, and all the other components have a glossy texture, reinforcing the new millennium theme.

In the Balance
Prudence Hammett

Opposite, earth is held aloft on abstract hands rising from a metal base that was commissioned by the arranger. The abstract feeling continues in the globe, which does not depict the continents but rather suggests geographical terrain and texture.

Normally pavé is a flat, two-dimensional technique, but here it is given a third dimension with mosses, lichens, and sedums applied to a twenty-four-inch Styrofoam ball. Tweezers, hot glue, and straight pins aided the careful placement of each variety, resulting in subtle contrasts and patterns that flow rhythmically across the surface.

A fascinating variety of textures in a limited palette compels the viewer to linger and contemplate. The arranger reminds us, "The earth's future is in our hands."

Suspended in Space
Gail Emmons

Figuring out how and why this floats in air is an acute challenge. With their monochromatic variety, a medley of orchids, anthuriums, bells of Ireland, poppy pods, and sculptural strelitzia leaves intrigues almost as much as the mysterious mechanics. The secret here lies in a narrow strip of clear Plexiglas barely visible as it supports this airborne design. What holds the strip? It is glued to a base of the same material that has been painted black to blend with the pedestal.

FROM THE EARTH
Jane Godshalk

Opposite, the cycle of life—
roots, branches, foliage, flowers,
seeds—is grounded on a base of
sand and springs from an earth-
colored container in a design
influenced by the European
modern mass style. Plant
materials are grouped for color
impact, while the roots and
branches add a sense of space to
the compact central mass. The
metallic blue of the mahonia
berries and cedar contrasts
with the brown and gold of the
roses, calla lilies, and hypericum
berries.

EXPLORATION AND DISCOVERY
Elvira M. Butz

With a manzanita branch found while hiking in Mexico, more than a dozen lichen and mosses collected in
Alaska, and sculptural rocks carried home over the years, the arranger has painted a picture of a verdant valley.
The new red growth in the twisted manzanita branch is echoed in the brilliant Humboldt lilies, the pincushion
proteas, bouvardias, kalanchoes, and hypericums.

The arranger's passion for the simpler forms in the plant kingdom—moss, lichen, fern—led to an in-depth
study of specimens collected near Fairbanks at the end of a trip to the Arctic Circle. She seconds the words of
E. M. Dunham, who wrote in 1916, "If it were not for the mosses, it is difficult to say how barren the woods
would be or how much beauty would be lost to Nature."

ANCHORED TO EARTH
Martha N. McClellan

The sturdy trunk of this floral tree is indeed a piece of tree trunk, smoothed and mellowed with age. It supports a tray containing eight blocks of Oasis that in turn holds more than a hundred Terra Cotta and Leonidas roses. The roses' coppery tones carry the eye across the mound and contrast with the yellow-greens of euphorbias, bells of Ireland, and Lenten roses. Foliage from east Tennessee gardens complete the picture—coral bells, pachysandra, red maple, galax, lamb's ears, epimedium, and China fir.

The blocking of colors was inspired by European modern mass designs and by the way floral carpets in church flower festivals are created. There, the center aisle of a church is lined with shallow trays filled with Oasis. Masses of flowers are cut short and placed close together to form patterns, similar to the bedding-out practice of Victorian times or the pavé technique.

Earth Tones
Sherran Blair

Subtle coloring and a variety of textures are the hallmarks of this intriguing design. The arranger has achieved a multilevel effect with a zigzag of driftwood that supports dark and light forms of fungi. The spiky haworthia contrasts with the rounded fungi and with the other succulent, aeonium.

The two aeonia grew on the arranger's windowsill before being beheaded for the flower show. The haworthia was taken from its pot to do duty in the arrangement. Interestingly, both plants survived the experience. The haworthia continues to grow on a piece of lava rock and the aeonia have sprouted new roots.

East Wind
Sandra S. Baylor

This six-foot-tall piece of wood from a swamp on the Eastern Shore of Virginia leaves no doubt that a powerful wind continues to blow. No longer upright, this tree with its weathered silvery surface tells a story of many seasons on a windy shore. Bits of Spanish moss manage to cling to balls of twigs, while queen proteas hug the trunk and reinforce the strong directional line of this design.

MOVING IN SPACE
Carol F. Critchlow

Space contained and space exploded was the concept this designer wanted to convey. A vase stand elevates large wood embroidery hoops whose crossing circles suggest orbital rotations as do loops of bear grass. In the center is a "big bang"—red roses, proteas, and pineapples—that explodes, sending comets of curly willow into outer space.

Following the Sun
Ingrid Kelly

The rhythm of rotation; the familiarity of a clock face; hot colors shooting out in solar flares—all of these elements communicate sun to the viewer. But a closer look at this arrangement will reveal some very down-to-earth components—a rusty jack stand, a rim of a wheel, a circular saw blade. These were found when the arranger took a wrong but fortuitous turn into the driveway of a junk shop. Research into folk art led to this framework, with metal dowels supporting the heavy saw blade and the rim mounted on the jack stand.

The saw blade holds a hand-tied arrangement of bromeliads that echo the colors of the rusted metal and the yellow-to-red of the sun. Circles cut from wood and painted red-orange are bolted to existing holes in the rim and rotated slightly, giving movement and depth. Two lengths of piano wire, inserted crosswise through the base of each pincushion protea, are threaded into holes drilled in the rings. Loops of liriope enclose space, counter flatness, and add rhythm and movement to the design.

FLAMES RISING
Leontine LaPointe

Heliconia and bird of paradise blossoms flicker through the wisps of Japanese broom in this transparent, freestyle design, opposite. They all leap out of a three-part container—stainless-steel cylinders torched at a high temperature to create a blistered texture and a blackened, perforated pattern. The tongues of broom escaping through the pierced openings make this interpretation of *fire* especially convincing.

ETERNAL FLAME
Nancy Ladd

Fire was precious in ancient Greece and Rome, so an ever-burning bowl was kept in the center of town. A two-foot-tall, Neoclassical container had the elegance and drama needed for this concept. Red-hot tropicals, curving palm fronds sprayed red, and papyrus—dried, clipped, and sprayed—leave no doubt that this torch is ablaze. Other modern touches—rolled leaves and freestanding heliconia at the base—move the arrangement from a traditional mass to a freestyle design.

Burning Low
Bonny Martin

Only the last flickering flames and a few glowing coals remain of what was once a roaring fire. This is the picture painted in skeletonized magnolia leaves, burgundy anthurium, and orange lichen on a marvelous twist of charred wood.

    The wood—from a dead Ponderosa pine found in Colorado—was given to the arranger years ago. A tip from Charles Kinnear, a South African floral designer—to paint the wood with paint thinner before applying a blowtorch—helped create the charred effect. (A garden hose was kept close at hand.)

Glowing Embers
Tricia Saul

A deliberate burn of an old, unsafe barn produced the components for this interpretation of fire, opposite. The corrugated roofing and the barn siding were transformed by the heat—altered in color, texture, and shape. The glossy black satin of the charcoaled wood contrasts with the soot-covered surface of the metal. A few flame-colored flowers— garden-grown irises, roses, and sparks of gloriosa lilies— emerge from the crumpled ruins, giving life to an otherwise desolate scene.

"I've Gone Native Now"
Bobbie Slater and Leslie Mattice

"Mahalo (thank you) for removing your shoes" is a common plaque on doorways in Hawaii. If you attend a large party or luau in Hawaii, there will be a tangle of shoes and slippers at the doors. At the end of the night you will hear, "Eh, who's got my other slipper?" echoing through the fragrant night air.

The slippers pictured here were cut from Oasis and the sides edged with a strip of ti leaf—first ironed to make it pliable. The thongs are made the way ti leaf leis are—strips of ti ironed, then twisted together. They are attached to the floral foam base with hot glue.

The biggest challenge for the arrangers was finding diminutive plant material in this land of six-foot-tall gingers and heliconia. Mums, rosebuds, and hydrangea petals filled the bill—and the slippers.

"I've Gone Native Now"
Barbara Masumoto and Dotty Nitta

The charge here was for a pavé arrangement representing a "local" object. Since the flower show was in Hawaii, what could be more local than the state fish, the humuhumu-nukunuku-a-pua'a?

How do you carve a fish shape from Oasis? The answer was in the denser designer block foam, which could withstand the weight of the water and flowers for the four days of the show. After many trial runs, flowers and ground cover blossoms from neighboring backyards proved the best survivors—marguerites, epidendrum orchids, mini garden mums, Dahlberg daisies, with baby wood roses for the eyes. The lines between blocks of color were drawn with painted, dried cloves; rhapis palm served for fins; and sago palm fluttered as eyelashes.

To Fly a Kite
Angeline F. Austin

Waves of red roses, purple statice, yellow carnations, and multicolored chrysanthemums move across this kite that rises above its pedestal, suggesting the power of the wind. The pattern was first drawn on paper, then flowers were placed according to the European technique of pavé. A one-inch-deep tray of sheet metal filled with wet floral foam holds the hundreds of flowers.

Shooting Star
Claire Ellis

Starlike lilies, orange and yellow proteas, bromeliads, and clipped palms spring from a core of fiery alstroemerias and shoot through space. A trail of pincushion mums and cocoa lashings marks their path. The fishing line that centers and stabilizes the floral component is barely visible, tied with a fly fisherman's skills from a cage of floral foam to three hooks on the iron star. Poised on point, its meteor magically suspended, this star suggests something far more ethereal than its thirty-two pounds.

TRIANGLES—OPEN AND CLOSED
Gail Emmons

A triangular container with a tight massing of iris and freesia is balanced by an inverted triangle of purple branches. A horizontal branch cuts across the design, uniting the elements, enclosing space, and creating tension.

MINERAL
Susan Detjens

This arrangement, opposite, was created for a flower show entitled "The Millennium: As It Was, Is, May Be." These words provided inspiration for a vertical design with corroded metal at the base (yesterday), moving into undulations of copper flashing (today), and ending at the top with subtle coils of coppery mesh (tomorrow). The verdigris of rex begonia leaves contrasts with the corroded copper, while the smooth texture of callas emphasizes the gloss of the new metal. Peach-colored foxtail lilies and curly willow carry the eye through the swirl of mesh.

The designer, who is a landscape painter, says, "I am always trying to create three dimensions on canvas with brushes and paint. It is exciting to work in three dimensions with found materials to tell a story, suggest a theme, and then to enrich this theme with plant material. The problem, the challenge of how to solve it, is totally absorbing and a lot of fun."

MASS AND SPACE
Margaret Pengilly

Years of ikebana study and an intriguing lecture by a French flower arranger resulted in this arrangement, which combines ideas about enclosed space and the massing of flowers. The Lucite stand aids the illusion of space so emphasis could be placed on the graceful line and textural contrast between the smooth, ribbonlike flax and the velvety celosia.

STRUGGLE FOR SPACE
Nancy D'Oench

Years ago this bittersweet vine, opposite, reached out to a young sapling, slowly but surely strangled it, then moved on in search of other prey. Now a bold banana blossom is an able adversary. The tension between the two strong forms invites the eye to see the spiraling of the vine repeated in the rotation of the young banana fingers around the upright stalk. Inflorescence of palm, artichokes, poppy pods, and black kangaroo paws contribute to the exotic feeling.

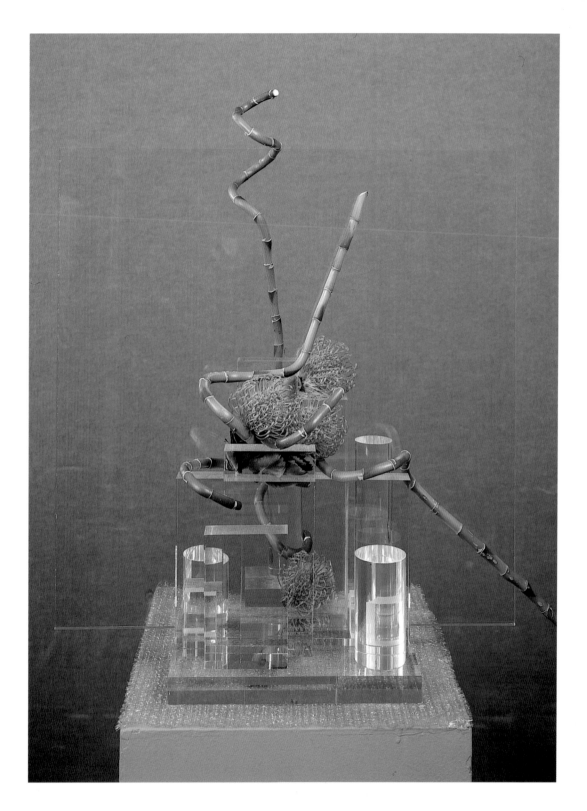

WATER
Sally Humphreys

Blocks and cylinders of Lucite on retreating planes create a sense of depth and suggest water at multiple levels. None exists, but the protea "submerged" behind a Lucite panel teases with the possibility. Lucky bamboo (trained dracaena) moves in and out of the design.

Illusion achieved, the arranger checks off the elements of design that have come into play—line, form, color, and texture—and the principles that contribute to the success of the composition—balance, contrast, rhythm.

"BEYOND THE REEF"
Patsy L. Gibson and
Pat Schnack

One line of the song "Beyond the Reef" says, "I'll send my lonely heart, for I love her so." Developing this idea, a coil of weathered copper tubing, opposite, holds heart-shaped, pink and green obake anthuriums, grown in Hawaii. Their path passes a mesquite branch that resembles black coral, pink and black sea fans, and glass balls, resting on the ocean floor beyond the reef. The pedestal, painted and covered with sand, unifies the components and heightens the textural quality of the composition.

TOOLSHED
Margaret Pengilly

On a well-worn workbench, the curve and texture of an electrical conduit is repeated in the loops and line of aspidistra leaves. The technique of splitting one side of the leaf at regular intervals and threading the pieces into the other side was learned at a workshop on modern Italian design with Carla Barbaglia.

In this interpretation of a "Toolshed," energy snakes through the leaves, conduit, vice, and pipe and explodes in a fireworks display of dried and painted allium.

"Beyond the Reef"
Tad Sewell and Sally Moore

"Cut" was the first thing this team did when they picked up their pedestal—cut off the top, cut open the front, cut out areas around the sides and back, opposite. Aiming to interpret an old Hawaiian song entitled "Beyond the Reef," their goal was to produce multiple layers of reef, summoning the second line of the title song, "where the sea is dark and cold."

A bit of light installed in the depth of the "reef" reveals numerous deep-sea phenomena rendered in plant material and a pavé of red rose petals between layers of Lucite. The inside, outside, and top of the pedestal are covered with papier-mâché and painted shades of blue, as are the two dowels that rise to heights of five and seven feet. Glossy heliconia "fish" swim by at eye level, contrasting with the reef's rough texture and convincing the viewer that this is indeed "beyond the reef."

"Beyond the Reef"
Bertie Lee and
Anna Lise Dyhr Vogel

A cornucopia of oceanic treasure spills out of a monk's drinking vessel, perhaps left on the seafloor centuries ago. Pincushion proteas and chartreuse and yellow orchids glow against the midnight blue of the pedestal. Glossy spider lily seed pods in green and burgundy reflect light and contrast with the rough textures of the other components.

An undulating length of vine wends its way around the vessel, across and down the pedestal. Is it the tentacle of a sea creature, a twisted bit of shipwreck, or a botanical marvel that grows only in the depths of eternal night?

FENCED IN
Cindy Affleck and Anna Smith

The Dadaists added a degree of realism to their abstract art, and that is what this team sought to do in their interpretaton of "Fenced In." The two set out across the Pennsylvania countryside in search of weathered wood planks and rusty hinges. The components, many of them actual fence parts, are not logically arranged but still assert their original character. A single heliconia with rusty shading on its stem adds a touch of life and continues the sculptural quality. The whole is supported by a steel rod that rises from a slanted platform, contributing to the feeling of suspension.

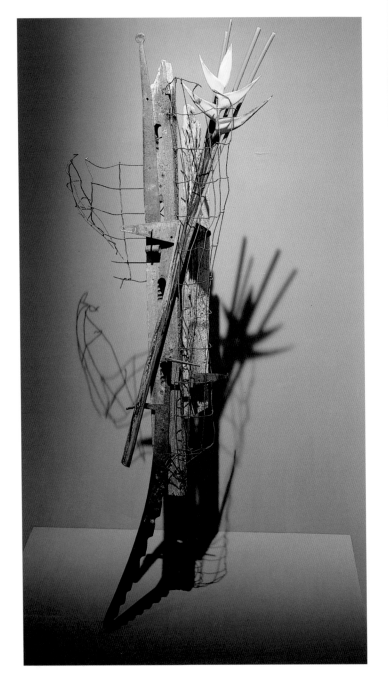

BRUSHSTROKES
Bonnie Schorsch and Shelley Schorsch

In addition to interpreting the title, "Brushstrokes," these arrangers were required to include an easel in their design. Not wanting to use the obvious artist's easel, they sought alternatives and found inspiration in a book of contemporary French flower arrangements. One design in the book incorporated a piece of Plexiglas, with plant material placed on both sides of it. If plant material were mounted on both sides of a large sheet of Plexiglas, it would create depth and give the impression of overlapping brushstrokes.

Palmetto palm was the plant material of choice, suggesting the shape of both brush and brushstrokes. Vibrant red gerbera daisies, pavéd on Oasis in a chicken-wire frame, are made all the redder by the direct color complement of chartreuse mums. Palms and frame are held securely in place by fine wire threaded through tiny holes in the sheet. Several feet of plastic tubing filled with green-colored water snakes through the design, recording the brush's path and uniting all elements.

SEA DREAMS
Tanya Alston and Ele Potts

A lone jellyfish with tentacles reaching to seven feet floats on the surface of this sea dream. Crisp dendrobium orchids in tiny vials, silvery Spanish moss, and prickly globe amaranths—pink, lavender, and white—cling to the fish-line tentacles, varying the texture while harmonizing with the iridescence above.

The supporting structure of this dreamlike creature is a Lucite dome filled with crushed iridescent paper. A Lucite circle, drilled with holes, fits under the dome and is threaded with shreds of paper and the fish line that holds the orchids and globe amaranths. A line runs from the center of the circle through the dome to an S-hook that is suspended from the ceiling.

A TRIBUTE TO JOHNNY APPLESEED
The Garden Club of Trenton

The overall theme of the 2001 Philadelphia Flower Show was Great Gardeners of the World, and this group of designers took as its inspiration and focus the gardener who created orchards in the wildernesses of Pennsylvania, Ohio, Kentucky, Illinois, and Indiana— John Chapman, a.k.a. Johnny Appleseed, opposite.

Research showed that he seldom slept indoors but did occasionally take shelter with settlers. The designers' challenge was to suggest a room in a log cabin, yet place the emphasis upon their subject's lifelong work—planting orchards. Transparent theatrical scrim offered the solution. Cabin "logs," constructed of hardware cloth only partially covered with papier-mâché bark, allow the scene of the orchard painted on a screen to show through. The scene is set for an arrangement that tells the story—from seed to fruit—of the first apple trees. On a makeshift pedestal of apple crates, amaryllis and forced branches of apple suggest the flowering of the trees, while round, green viburnum blossoms cascade over the crates, much as a heavily laden branch of green apples would. Grapevines lead the eye to the soil—point of entry for the "apple seeds" that follow its path. These "seeds" are coffee beans hot-glued to thin filament and loosely strung down the vines.

The headline "First Apple Blossoms" heralds the success of Chapman and of this project, which engaged two-thirds of the club's members.

Chapter 7   Floral Fashions—Botanic Couture

Costume galleries in museums recognize the artistic value of clothing and offer a change of pace to the visitor. In this chapter we do the same. Here we feature fashion—actual couture gowns complemented by flower arrangements; chapeaux fashioned from unlikely fabrics—celosias, palm fronds, and billy balls; and jewelry to decorate the décolletage of a socialite. All salute the talent of the couturier and the flower arranger.

GOWNS FOR THE GALA

Fashion speaks a universal language. The elegance of line, the allure of texture, the subtleties of contrast, all exert their appeal. Here, arrangers complement designs by American couturiers with equally artistic arrangements, capturing in plant material the pattern, line, and texture of the gowns.

Worn in the USA
Isabel Morian Lamb

Sago palm fronds repeat the scallops on the bodice and the pattern in the fabric of this elegant gown by American designer Pauline Trigère. The phalaenopsis orchids and the voids created by the loops of palm echo the white that peeks through the leaf pattern on the dress. The container, a sculpture done years earlier by the arranger's mother, continues the simple but bold feeling of this Rousseauesque design.

Worn in the USA
Nancy Godshall

What do you use to complement a San Carlin evening gown in black velvet and copper satin? This arranger focused on the diagonal line in the gown torso, the rhythm, volume, and swirl of the skirt, and the contrasting textures of the soft velvet and the shiny satin. A topiary frame captures the swirl of the skirt, and coppery Leonidas roses continue the rotating direction, leading the eye to the strong diagonal of a *Strelitzia nicolai*—a large bird of paradise relative with white flowers rising from a blue-gray boat. Loops of aspidistra leaves provide a contrast of texture, just as the satin does in the gown.

Worn in the USA
Ann Heist

The luxurious fullness of this navy blue gown by the Haitian-born American designer Fabrice is interpreted in a traditional mass design. The urn-shaped container recalls the silhouette of the garment and adds its own classical touch. Roses and lilies in warm tones, blue irises, glistening red hypericum pods, and arches of foliage capture the color and glint of the beads and pearls on the bodice and peplum.

HATS THAT TURN HEADS

If there is one class in a flower show guaranteed to bring smiles to visitors' faces, it is the hat class. The familiarity of the form, the incongruity of wearing leaves and lichen, the delight that a well-designed hat always brings to the eye—whatever it is, it is sure to please.

The search for material in this enterprise focuses on plants that can hold up to serious manipulation and withstand heat and transportation. With tools and plant material assembled, the real creativity begins. "I wanted my hats to have an almost fabriclike quality," explains designer Mari Tischenko, "and to use leaves and flowers that would create the *illusion* of a feather, velvet, pompom, pleat, or veil. Cockscomb, for example, looks and feels like deep, rich velvet mouton. When I shredded the flax leaf it became a veil. One of my friends was convinced that the 'feather' on my pillbox was indeed a real feather."

HATS (Opposite)
Sally Chapman, Mari Tischenko, Sally Chapman (left to right)

Protea: Ready for a garden party—or a garden club meeting in the 1930s—this creation of aspidistra and flax is accented front and center with a sunburst of pincushion protea.

Cockscomb: In shades of burgundy and chartreuse, cockscomb communicates the warmth of Persian lamb. Aspidistra hugs the head while a leaf of strelitzia erases any prospect of stuffiness.

Flower lei: When this arranger was in Hawaii to judge the Honolulu Flower Show, she bought a lei and eventually dried it with silica gel. Here it adorns a crisp brim of aspidistra leaves, accented with green raffia and "feathers" cut from leaves.

HATS
Mari Tischenko, Ellie Gardner, Sally Chapman (left to right)

Feather: The feather is a young sago palm frond, anchored by a trio of billy balls and pinned to ribbons of ti leaves and variegated flax. The veil is a shredded flax leaf.

Bird in the hat: A very fashionable bird clothed in hydrangea petals sits atop a nest of pittosporum, geranium leaves, and green mums protected by a bit of oak branch. Red maple seeds and "smoke" from the smoke tree add sparks of color.

Bird of paradise: This elegant swirl of aspidistra leaves, highlighted by a bird of paradise blossom, is reminiscent of a 1940s dinner hat.

Hat on the Horizontal
Jane Kilduff

Sophisticated and refined; was this worn by Audrey Hepburn in one of her movies?

The beautifully lacquered surface still reveals the outline and texture of the ti leaves on the crown and the magnolia leaves covering the brim. The line of the brim is interrupted by veiling woven from bear grass, permitting the wearer to see and be seen. Fresh multicolored anthurium, precisely trimmed, adorn this Paris-inspired creation.

Vertical View
Julie Lapham

Here's a hat, opposite, with attitude—and with bold line, rhythmic balance, subtle coloring, and dramatic textural contrasts.

Two succulents form the focal area and anchor the sweep of motion created by the clipped areca palm. Galax leaves, fungi, and wisps of fern vary the textural quality while limiting the color palette. The entire arrangement rests in an Oasis cage wired to the top of the wicker form.

DESIGNING WITH NATURE'S JEWELS

Since 1996 a section that has been very popular at the Philadelphia Flower Show is jewelry. Beautifully lighted and displayed in secured cases worthy of the real thing, this jewelry, incredibly, is made entirely of dried plant material. It's a design challenge that combines creativity, craftsmanship, and problem-solving on an intimate scale.

IN A SPLIT SECOND
Alice Hamilton Farley

A snake you wouldn't mind having around your neck is captured at the split second his tongue—two pieces of cedrela seedpod—flicks out of his brazil-nut mouth. This sinuous, contemporary creature is covered with tiny pieces of oak leaves cut into a diamond pattern, which are in turn overlaid with real gold leaf. The "carnelian" inlay is made of yards and yards of liriope leaves sliced into strips and coated with nail polish. A few well-placed millet seeds accent the snake's jewel-like head.

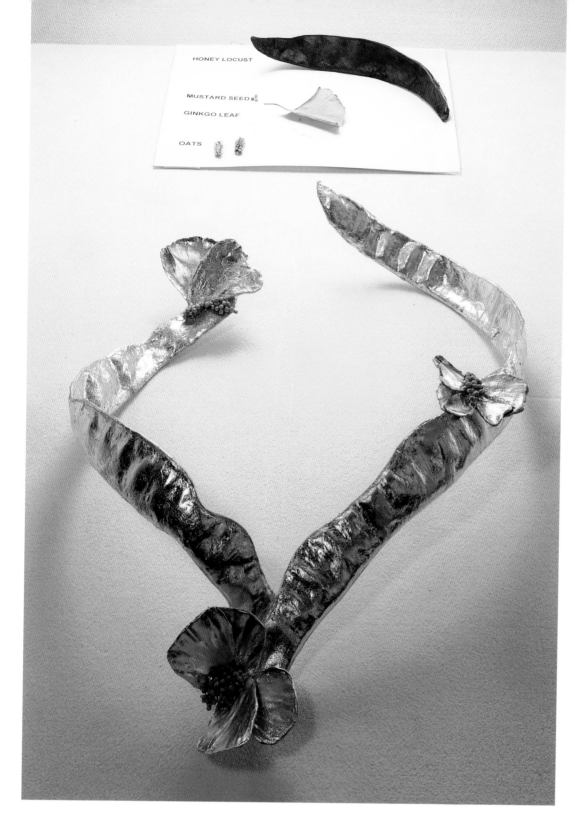

IN A SPLIT SECOND
Ginny Simonin

Surely this design in a window on Fifth Avenue would stop shoppers in their tracks. The sculptural honey locust pods, gilded in silver and gold, appear ready to grace the décolletage of a ball gown. Butterflies, fashioned from ginkgo leaves, light on the pods.

AN ARRANGER'S PERSPECTIVE

Alice Hamilton Farley has won the Philadelphia Horticultural Society Grand Sweepstakes Trophy three times for her participation in a broad range of classes—jewelry, pressed-plant creations, flower arranging, horticulture.

This arranger normally works on a larger scale; she's a landscape architect—but clearly she excels at small-scale challenges as well. Farley's perspective on the creative process is interesting. "Usually, I go easy on research per se," she says. "I will read a bit about a style, period, or artist, but I want inspiration, not to copy specific historical examples.

If I am really stumped, I often turn to a wonderful book, *La France et ses Bouquets*. I particularly relish the inventive way that foliage is used to create rhythm and movement and the spare yet lush and complex feel to the designs. I also refer to a great little book by Herbert Read, *Modern Sculpture*. It is chock-full of interesting forms and shapes.

"Once I am done, I walk away happily. I never worry about the judges or the judging process and I don't get in a tizzy over the judging results. The judges will like my effort—for the same reasons I do or for other reasons—or they will not like it. Their comments interest me though. Often they find the weak spots that I had hoped they wouldn't notice."

NUTMEG

MUSTARD SEED

MUNG BEAN

SOYBEAN

WILLOW

HULLED MILLET

ARBORIO RICE

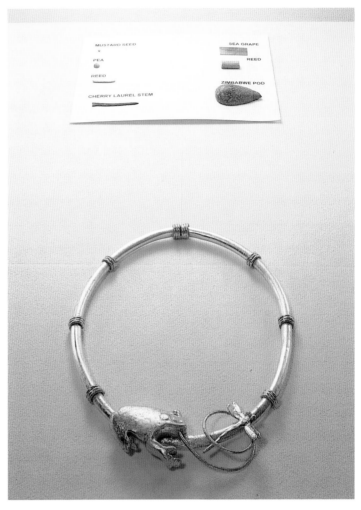

IN A SPLIT SECOND
Jane Vanderzee

With the elegance of crown jewels and the intricacy of millefleur, thirty carved nutmegs, opposite, are encrusted with seeds and centered by "lapis" soybean gemstones. The unicorn pendant, caught leaping in flight, is pieced together with razor-thin slices of balsa wood and covered with layers of mustard seed, millet, mung beans, and arborio rice. Willow serves as the horn, the clasp, and the connector to the pendant.

IN A SPLIT SECOND
Dottie Sheffield

In a split second, right, a frog wraps its tongue around a dragonfly; or, to translate that into plant material, a zimbabwe pod with a split-pea eye extends a length of tiny reed around a cherry laurel stem with mustard-seed eyes and sea-grape wings. The necklace itself is fashioned from heavier reed, soaked, then coaxed into shape on a board within a frame of nails, and left to dry. Silver and gold leaf provide the luster.

ABOUT TO TAKE WING
Betty Davis

This dragonfly would be welcome in any garden or on any gown. Its wings—carefully trimmed galax leaves—are from the garden, as is the Texas mountain laurel seedpod that forms part of the body. The eyes and nose were made from American elm seeds. The remainder, lentils and split peas, are from the grocery store.

Chapter 8   Museums—Fine Art with Flowers

With events named "Art in Bloom," "Bouquets to Art," and "Fine Art and Flowers," museums across the country celebrate their collections and the fine art of flower arranging. These events delight arrangers, viewers, and museums alike. The arranger is motivated to study a work of art in depth, researching the artist, the period, and the style, something most museumgoers would enjoy doing but seldom can. The visitor is rewarded with a breathtaking display of flower arrangements and attractions such as demonstrations, speakers, book signings, festive luncheons, and boutiques.

The museum is perhaps the greatest beneficiary. Attendance escalates on the flower show days; people who have never crossed the threshold before come to see the flowers and are introduced to the museum's treasures. Viewers linger in front of each work of art much longer than they normally would, pausing to see what the arranger saw, trying to figure out which line or color or texture led to a particular interpretation, discussing the components with their friends. And the flower shows and "Art in Bloom" events make money for the institutions. Boston's Museum of Fine Arts was the first to institute "Art in Bloom," a title and format that have been picked up by museums across the country. Begun in 1976, this event now nets approximately $400,000 a year. The Wadsworth Atheneum in Hartford, Connecticut, the oldest museum in continuous operation in America, has been hosting "Fine Art and Flowers" since 1981; the proceeds make possible fresh flowers throughout the museum the rest of the year.

Many arrangers consider "Art in Bloom" exhibitions the most rewarding arranging they do. Participation provides the impetus to become immersed in an artwork, to look at a piece of art for its design qualities, as well as for its historical and sociological implications. How is the space divided? Is that the golden mean? How can that wonderful texture be spotlighted, that color captured? What will show the excitement of this artwork without copying it?

On the following pages is a sampling of flower arrangements that interpret and complement the fine art on view in museums. The elements and principles of design continue to govern flower arranging in museums as they do in all other venues. There are, however, additional guidelines that influence thinking about these art-inspired projects. To start, arrangers stay away from repainting the picture, and avoid trying to replicate every

line and color of the artwork in plant material. Instead, they abstract one or more elements from the artwork, and let that lead their thinking. If the most striking component is the strong line of a figure or a color, that element is emphasized in the design.

It is the spirit of the work of art that the arranger tries to capture, and this may or may not be done in the style of the original. A contemporary style will most likely be employed to interpret a Pablo Picasso painting; a John Singer Sargent portrait will probably be complemented by an elegant mass design, but not necessarily. Arrangers look at the artwork as they look at plant material, studying it for color, three-dimensional forms, dominant lines, textures, open and enclosed spaces, and size. This last element is of prime consideration. The size and feel of the painting is reflected both in the actual size of the arrangement and in the visual weight of the design. There is a synergy between the work of art and the successful flower arrangement, leading the eye back and forth.

On the following pages, arrangers invite you to look closely at a work of art and at the companion flower arrangement, to see what they see.

THE CONTEST BETWEEN
APOLLO AND MARSYAS
BY TINTORETTO
Cathie Pike and Cecilie Cruger

A classical container and bold plant material capture the scale, rhythm, and color of this masterpiece. Each variety—anthuriums with red, pink, and beehive gingers massed in the modern style—echoes a block of color in the painting. A wisteria vine, dancing to the music of the violin, enlarges the design and lightens it at the same time, enclosing negative space.

STANDING FIGURE OF A GODDESS
Lucy Belding

The strong verticality, the pattern and texture of the statue are abstracted by the designer and translated into plant material—upright bamboo, pleated palm, and curving callas. Strelitzia leaves continue the vertical thrust.

A floor lamp (*sans* wiring) is the core of this construction, circled by Oldhami bamboo, and topped by a container fashioned from aluminum flashing. The faux limestone base has a hole in the center, permitting it to be threaded over the lamp rod. Pieces of broken "limestone" add to the feeling of antiquity.

MADONNA AND CHILD WITH SAINTS JANUARIUS AND SEBASTIAN
BY FRANCESCO SOLIMENA
Nina Hayssen

A horizontal design with a strong central focus complements the bilateral symmetry of the icon, with saints on either side of the Virgin and Christ. Yarrow, curly dock, cattails, and rubber plant leaves, turned to show the brown underside, reflect the gold and brown of the painting, as does the brass container, which is elevated on a base similar to the squares beneath the saints.

Masses of pink carnations and red alstroemerias reflect the religious fervor of the medieval period, the whole taking on the form of a crucifix.

THE EGGSELLER BY FRANÇOIS BOUCHER
Sheila Graham-Smith

The thematic elements of protection and vulnerability in the painting are evident in this intriguing arrangement. Pandanus "eggs" are embraced by "arms" of forsythia, the oval construction repeating the shape of the framing and the eggs in the picture.

Though egg-shaped, the pandanus looks armored, not vulnerable, leaving the viewer with a question. The painting, too, leaves the viewer wondering where the main interest of the buyer lies and just what should be protected.

The leucadendrons and kangaroo paws were chosen to echo the reds and creams of the painting and possibly, by their shapes, to hint at the erotic tension of the painting.

MADONNA AND CHILD BY NARDO DI CIONE
Judith Stark

With its halolike circles, strong color combinations, and ethereal elevation, the aesthetic and the spiritual meet in this flower arrangement. The elevated container is the work of a plumber who accepted the challenge of fabricating a stand from copper pipes and flashing. The copper is continued in halos of tubing, and the color is echoed in the warm tones of the lilies, roses, and crocosmias. Hosta leaves repeat the shape of the frame and blue irises offer contrasts in color, form, and texture.

THE TWO MAJESTIES BY JEAN-LÉON GÉRÔME
Cato Schley

Opposite, an arrangement of appropriately named Leonidas roses with yellow and orange callas is indeed regal in its posture as it leads the eye to the sun and the lion in the painting. A piece of red granite reflects the colors of the sky while suggesting the weight of the rocky cliff, and golden amaranthus extends the visual path in this line-mass design.

The arranger, who chose the painting because it had long been a favorite, observed, "Gérôme mastered the element of light in his painting just as nature has done with flowers. They are never flat, but full of life and light."

THE HERD BOY BY FREDERIC REMINGTON
Laura Gregg and Lani McCall

A chill sweeps over the viewer approaching these two works. Even from a distance, the bitter cold wind is palpable, the hardship of survival painful. As the viewer draws nearer, the subtleties and contrasts of color and texture in the depth of the design become evident. Flowers, mosses, and fungi echo the colors and textures in the painting while communicating the frigid peril of the herd boy.

From October, when they signed up for the class, until the show in April, this team looked for containers, plant material, and ways to interpret the bone-chilling wind of Remington's painting. A branch of magnolia, picked up after an ice storm, proved to have the horizontal motion and rough beauty they sought.

The synergy between the painting and the arrangement is extraordinary, moving the eye back and forth and making the impact of the combination greater than the sum of the parts.

Banksia serrata BY PAUL JONES
Bonny Martin

Two hollow cycad stems, purchased in the flower market in New York in 1966 and stored for future use, repeat the shape of the protea blossom gone to seed depicted in the watercolor. The seeds are represented in the arrangement by small, polished river rocks. A black wrought-iron stand supports the silvered piece of driftwood, which, in turn, holds the pieces of cycad at two levels. Two stems of regal slipper orchids, *Paphiopedilum*, emerge from floral foam in the cycads' hollow centers and bring the design to life.

The whole composition is poised on an almost invisible point, creating a sense of suspension reminiscent of the inverted blossom in the watercolor. The class description asked for "Natural images creating balance." Request fulfilled.

LEAF BY SUE HERBERT
Margot Paddock

Brown calathea leaves echo the silhouette in Herbert's watercolor, while green anthuriums and lotus pods, luminous in the museum lighting, suggest the breaks in the decomposing leaf's structure. Costus sticks form the spine, giving visual and physical support to the other components.

Here, a flat leaf is interpreted with depth, drama, and movement. The original is suspended in space; the arrangement floats in its container above the pedestal.

ARTICHOKE FLOWER BY BRIGID EDWARDS
Helen Goddard

Opposite, the structure of the artichoke—its bold stem and explosive florescence—gains new emphasis when inverted in the flower arrangement. A blue-tinted mirror compounds the depth, suggesting the aerodynamic liftoff of a rocket.

The bundled equisetum captures the texture, strength, and color of the artichoke stem, while groupings of leucadendrons, calla lilies, and blue throatworts suggest the layers of the opening blossom. Bundling, massing, and the clean, bold shape are all typical of modern Italian design.

CYCAD BY LESLIE CAROL BERGE
Jenny Lynn Bradley and Claire Ellis

Sago palm from Savannah yards and cabbage palm that grows wild in Georgia marshes capture the drama of this watercolor. Bright red ginger blossoms represent the female cones of the cycad *Encephalartos ferox* and a collar of copper roof flashing repeats and exaggerates the color and shape of the surrounding leaflets. The clipped cabbage palm leaves recall the two dark fronds in the watercolor, and swirls of sago palm give the design rhythm and depth.

The heavy plant material—a cabbage palm stem can be two inches across—has been carefully trimmed, taped, and supported on sticks. Balance is evident and essential. The color and form of the base repeat the copper of the leaflets and the lines of the sago palm. The dark underlay and off-center placement add to the drama.

Two Piece Marble by Barbara Hepworth
Maryjo Garre

With the restraint and simplicity of the sculptor, the arranger calls attention to mass and voids. Light reflecting off Lake Michigan, through windows of the Milwaukee Art Museum, illuminates the spaces in the sculpture and in the container, contrasting with the dark voids represented by the centers of the sunflowers.

The crinkled texture of the green hydrangea blossoms counters the smoothness of the marble while still suggesting, in its mazelike intricacy, an impenetrable mass.

The simplicity and purity of the sculpture dictated the arrangement. The design, the arranger said, was all about space—perceived, defined, created.

RACE BY OSKAR SCHLEMMER
Nancy D'Oench

Muscle for muscle, sinew for sinew, the curves of the bittersweet vine reproduce the sinuous undulations of the athlete's body. Glass columns supporting "heads" of flowers and a grid that is neither in the foreground nor background force the eye back to the painting where the planes confuse and intrigue.

Spheres of Oasis hold green cymbidium orchids, pincushion proteas, leucadendrons, spray roses, and hypericum berries. A Plexiglas base recalls the transparency in Schlemmer's work while concealing a sturdy iron base welded with a pipe to support the six-foot vine. Croton leaves conceal the pipe, repeat the colors of the painting, and begin the spiraling motion of the bittersweet vine.

THE FICKLENESS OF THE HEART BY RENÉ MAGRITTE
Nancy Ladd

One strong line, the trunk of the tree, is the backbone of Magritte's emotional painting and the core of this interpretive arrangement. A cedar post, representing the tree, is topped by a square container with fingerlike magnolia branches emerging from its center. An inverted heliconia "drips blood" across the line of three calla lilies, which recall the purity of the marble head. An oval stone leads the eye to the sphere behind the marble bust, while the black base unites the elements and anchors the composition, much as the dark ground in the painting does.

The arranger, an art consultant for corporations, takes particular delight in the imagination, symbolism, and even humor found in Surrealist works.

PROCESSION
BY NANCY CHEAIRS
Penny Horne

The shape of the stylized trees in the painting is immediately recognizable in this sculptural creation—but the textures are reversed. The bark of the trunk has been transplanted to the canopy, while the trunk has the sleekness of leaves. Loops of raffia repeat the loop of clothesline, and bicolored anthuriums and Green Goddess calla lilies recall the laundry shapes in the literal yet abstract painting.

Rising above bases of Lucite and mirror, a column of equisetum hugs a PVC pipe core and supports the egg-shaped treetop, rich in texture, intriguing in its broken surface and exposed interior. The egg shape provides a clue to the construction. Have you ever covered an inflated balloon with string that has been dipped in glue and liquid starch, allowed it to dry, and punctured the balloon, leaving the hollow "shell" of an egg? That's the beginning of this structure, with the added dimension of bark stripped from a tree and hot-glued to the surface.

Shelf fungi, collected from decaying trees, connect the top of the tree to the trunk and lead the eye to the flying lines of the callas and obake anthuriums.

PROCESSION
BY NANCY CHEAIRS

NUMBER 6
BY JACKSON POLLOCK
Margot Paddock

Brush-shaped anthuriums move across this black "canvas" with all the energy of Jackson Pollock's splatters, even exceeding the dimensions of their frame. The light-colored flowers leap out of the dark, receding background, creating tremendous depth just as Pollock did with multiple layers of paint.

CRYING GIRL
BY ROY LICHTENSTEIN
Gay Estes

From the shimmer of shade cloth on the base and the anthurium lips, to the tears suspended in space, this very contemporary line arrangement bemuses and beguiles. The arranger calls it "Turning on the Waterworks," a reference to the components found in the plumbing section of Lowe's Home Store—a length of pool hose, a drain cover, and a female pipe joint.

Two teardrop ornaments repeat the translucence and shape of the holes in the drain and lead the eye to the bubbles on the pedestal. They, in turn, send the eye back along the strong linear path.

GLOUCESTER HARBOR BY STUART DAVIS
Carol Swift

Opposite, the fractured colors of Stuart Davis's harbor scene suggested the blocks of color and light in this abstract interpretation. Multicolored sections of a CD rack let rectangles of light pass through while the orange, red, green, and blue of birds of paradise repeat the colors of the painting. Brown and gray are translated by clipped staghorn fern; a burst of red and green bromeliad varies the pattern. Plant material is secured with more strips of color—plastic clothespins.

At the base, rotating squares of Plexiglas, slightly separated, support the construction and hint at the existence of more slices of light.

LAKEISHA, JACKIE, AND CRYSTAL BY DAWOUD BEY
Sylvia Abbott

Dawoud Bey is a photographer known for his images of contemporary people of color. He produced this photograph of three students when he came to Hartford as artist-in-residence at the Wadsworth Atheneum in 1996.

The arranger translated the grid of the apartment window into a three-dimensional construction that holds three smooth pieces of weathered, intertwined manzanita, suggesting the intimate friendship of the three young women.

The grid and base are in the subdued mahogany tones of much of the photograph, but the three "Mango" calla lilies reflect the warm skin tones and the femininity and spirit of the subjects.

WALLDRAWING #612 BY SOL LEWITT
Kate Coley

The complete title of this installation by conceptual artist Sol LeWitt, opposite, is *Forms Derived from a Cubic Rectangle with Color Ink Washes Superimposed. Each is Bordered with a 10" (25 cm.) Color Ink Wash Band.*

Bands of "superimposed color ink washes" encircle an entire room of the Wadsworth Atheneum in Hartford, Connecticut. The washes are pure, primary-colored inks—red, yellow, and blue —plus gray, applied with a soft cloth, one layer at a time, in the number and sequence specified by the artist. The layers intermingle to create new hues directly on the wall.

The arranger has chosen a section of the room where borders of red and yellow meet in the corner, reproducing the angles of the room with a bamboo construction that also suggests another work by LeWitt, *Unfinished Cubes.* The bundles of equisetum, the dracaena, heliconia, and birds of paradise arranged on different planes recall the layers of ink while the broad banana leaves acknowledge the flat wall surface. Gradations of color are evident in the plant material and in the wall treatment.

HONOLULU ACADEMY OF THE ARTS
Betty Ho

Framing the wrought-iron doors to the Honolulu Academy of Arts are two ten-foot-tall flower arrangements overflowing with material that causes most visitors, including experienced flower arrangers, to gasp. Someone's *Agave americana*—century plant—has been severed from its roots, the yardlong, succulent leaves reassembled into mammoth arrangements. Contrasting with the silver of the agave is the red-violet of more than a hundred stems of dendrobium orchids.

"Harvesting" agave boggles the mind of most arrangers and gardeners, but plants grow very fast in Hawaii, particularly in Manoa, a section of Oahu known for its "Manoa mist." Anne Swanson of the Garden Club of Honolulu summed up the horticultural cycle with this Hawaiian saying, "Plant it one year. Enjoy it the second year. Take a machete to it the third year." Those machete leavings sometimes find a place of honor in the Academy.

The designer and executor of these two sculptures in plant material is Betty Ho, a twenty-five-year veteran of the volunteer corps that arrives at the academy every Monday morning to create flower arrangements from the luxuriant offerings of Hawaii's gardens and roadsides. Ho and the other volunteers are following a tradition begun by Caroline Peterson when the academy opened in 1927, and continued until recent years by May Moir. Moir's words still ring in arrangers' ears as they search for each week's components, "Scrounge! Train your eye . . . to see the full potential of a plant or a piece of driftwood or a cluster of flowers; you must train yourself to look for it. Once you learn to see beauty in the commonplace, the whole world looks better."

Chapter 9 Beyond the Walls—New Locations, Fresh Looks

The design of any arrangement and its success are determined in large part by its setting. An arrangement on the dining-room table, a bouquet in the guest bedroom, a flower in a bud vase in the powder room, all reflect the dictates of their surroundings. An arrangement placed on the floor of an entryway will be different from one placed on a mantel. Earlier we saw how designs in niches, on pedestals, and beside works of art respond to the space and style of adjoining components. But what happens when the surroundings of these arrangements change? Can design go beyond the walls, move to new locations?

In this section we see arrangements perform on new and different stages—from private gardens to public spaces to Elvis Presley's Graceland. Most of these designs were originally created for flower shows, but they take on a new dimension outside the walls of the exhibition space. In the following photographs, the art of the arrangement meets the art of the environment. The whole is definitely more than a sum of the parts.

GEOMETRIC ABSTRACT
Carol Henderson

This spare construction intrigues with its geometric forms—spheres, cubes, and triangles. The reeds and crown-of-thorns branches were acquired at a garden club meeting to which members brought unusual plant specimens to show and share. Wires inserted in the hollow reeds made it possible to bend them, enclosing triangular spaces. These lines, crossing with the lines in the wall, create even more triangles and rectangles. The spheres of dried yellow statice are complemented by the crown-of-thorns painted glossy purple.

RUGGED NORTHWEST
Ann Bucknall and Joy Nichols

Opposite, ascending curves of a tree fungus start the motion that leads to two towering peaks of slate, in reference to the ruggedness of the region. The Northwest theme is reinforced with plant material from the area—sword fern (*Polystichum munitum*), rhododendron (*Caucasicum x Ponticum varalbum*), and—visible just beyond the peak —lodge pole pine (*Pinus contorta*).

The diverse elements are compelling in their contrast— the gloss of the leaves against the rough stone—yet restrained and harmonious. William Carlos Williams talked about a poem as something that didn't have any extra parts in it. Here's a poem to the Northwest.

MOTION AND FORM
Carol Swift

A slight wind could lift this scoop of palm sheath, rustle the loquat leaves, and set the sago fronds in motion. Yet here, in the Cullen Sculpture Garden at the Museum of Fine Arts, Houston, the design bears a striking resemblance in form and color to the very solid Ellsworth Kelly sculpture in the background. The sheath hangs from an Oasis cage that sits atop a Plexiglas stand and holds a cluster of sea-blue agapanthus.

Steel Magnolias
Clover Earl

A sculpture commissioned by the arranger and loops of palm vividly convey the ups and downs, ins and outs of the mother-daughter relationship in Robert Harling's book *Steel Magnolias*. Contrasting textures, enclosed space, depth of field, asymmetrical balance—all engage the viewer. In the distance, a Frank Stella sculpture in the Cullen Sculpture Garden at the Museum of Fine Arts, Houston, echoes the powerful shape.

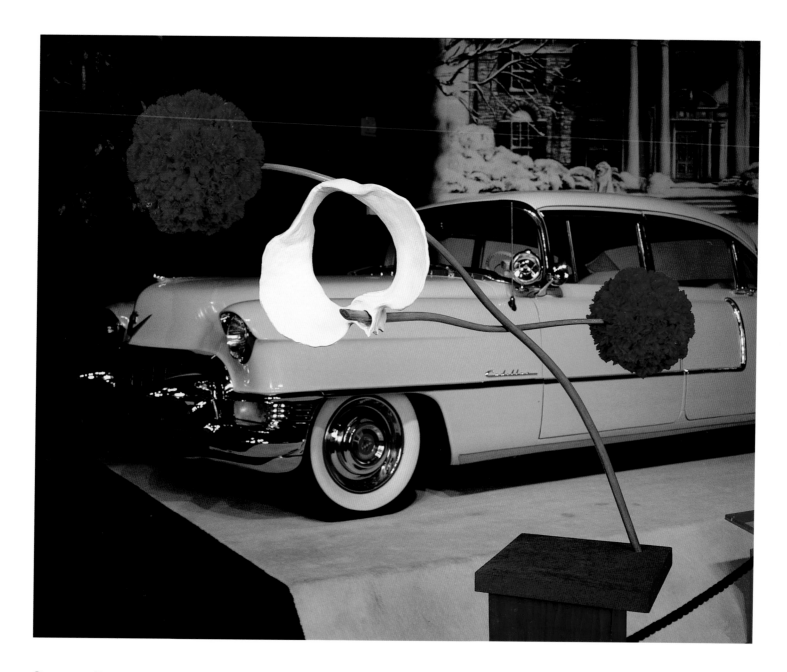

ROCK AND ROLL
Carol Mc Donald

Elvis Presley's pink Cadillac stands in the background, pristine and preserved at Graceland. In front of it is an abstract arrangement interpreting "Rock and Roll." The circle of the white-walled tire is repeated in the circular form in the arrangement; the soft pink of the paint is intensified in two pavé spheres of magenta carnations.

Catching the rhythm, the balance, the motion, and music of the rock-and-roll legend, this design teeters on the edge of a blue base weighted with a steel plate.

When this arranger was young, married with two children and finishing college, Elvis twice performed in her hometown of Monroe, Louisiana. She missed him both times; still regrets it. This was her way of making amends.

DESERT FREE STYLE
Carol Henderson

Reds and yellows, fresh flowers and bleached shells, smooth callas and rough stone walls all come together in this freestyle design set against the Nevada landscape. Inspired by a metal sculpture seen in California, and years of ikebana study, the arrangement plays the smooth regularity of the hula hoop against the free movement of fasciated asparagus. Calla lilies, warmed by hand, are shaped to follow the circle of the hoop, while king proteas echo the reds.

A clamp to the wooden base anchors the hoop, and pierced, weathered stones hold the twists of dried, painted asparagus in place. The ribbonlike asparagus is green and flexible when fresh and becomes yellowish brown and rigid when dried. The fresh pieces were curled over chairs and left to dry in the desired shape.

ENTANGLEMENTS
Susan Detjens and Pinkie Roe

This arrangement, opposite, was originally created for a class in the Philadelphia Flower Show called "Entanglement—A Design Using a Garden Hose." A black soaker hose offered dramatic color, a matte finish, and no-kink flexibility. With friends' helping hands, then masking tape, and finally wire covered with painted strings, the desired loops were secured and the spaces enclosed. It was suspended from two parallel bars with monofilament.

To emphasize the rhythm and for compatibility in scale and texture all that was needed was the dramatic blossom of white bird of paradise. White birds (*Strelitzia nicolai*) are a much larger form of the orange and blue *Strelitzia reginae*. Bluish black sheaths, more than a foot long, enclose white birdlike blossoms. Not readily available, some were finally located in Florida and shipped in zero-degree March weather.

Originally hung against a plain white background, here the rounded sculptural form contrasts with the shapes and textures of a Connecticut wall. The blue of the birds reflects the blue in the stone.

CROSSING LINES
Gail Emmons

A tripod supports thirty pieces of wood painted black and crisscrossed to form a sculpture that moves outward. The severity of the wood is countered by the lushness of dozens of obake anthuriums in red and green, and strelitzia and phormium leaves, springing from the core. The whole is set in motion by red strips of bamboo, circling the design.

This construction—disassembled, color coded for reconstruction, and packed into a hard-case golf bag—was shipped to Genoa where it represented the Garden Club of America in a flower show. Home again in the Bay Area, it was reconstructed in the Sunken Garden at Filoli.

RHYTHM AND REPETITION
Gail Emmons

The orange of pincushion proteas and spider orchids contrasts with the green of the bamboo. The verticality of the bamboo is repeated in the finer water reeds and in the columns of a rotunda reflected in the pool. Bamboo strips enclose space, repeat the roundness of the bamboo, and set the piece in motion, an illusion aided by the off-center placement of the bamboo on the triangular base.

MODERN AND HORIZONTAL
Helen Goddard

Monochromatic, horizontal, modern European mass—all of these terms apply to this design in green set on the edge of a pool at Tower Hill Botanic Garden in Boylston, Massachusetts.

The arranger says the horizontal style is her favorite, and encourages others to give it a try:

"As in other European mass arrangements, the plant material should be bold, dramatic, and of varying textures and shapes. One needs long stems and/or branches for a strong horizontal line and solid round forms for the focal point. The material is grouped or blocked, and there is no transitional material. Since this arrangement is monochromatic, the contrasts are in texture and form—echeverias with chrysanthemums, orchids with phormiums. The balance is visual and usually asymmetrical.

"The mechanics are not complicated; the Oasis just needs to extend several inches above the lip of the container so you can insert the stems horizontally. If using fairly heavy plant material, it helps to mold chicken wire around·the Oasis, then tape it to the lip of the container.

"Incidentally, echeverias can be used over and over again by replanting them between arrangements—Yankee thrift applied to a modern European style."

Eye on the Horizon
Nancy D'Oench

This horizontal design echoes the shapes and colors of the
Massachusetts countryside as seen from Tower Hill Botanic Garden.
The topography is repeated in the linear forms of sanseviera and bells
of Ireland; variegated loops of New Zealand flax (*phormium*) catch the
light of a lake; and dahlias tipped with purple lead the eye to clover
blossoms in the field. Hosta leaves accent the bold form and grey-
green of the container.

"Singin' in the Rain"
Sandra Patterson

Passers-by smile, then begin to hum, "Singin' in the rain, just . . ."

In Gene Kelly's dance sequence to the title song of "Singin' in the Rain," he cavorts in a rain-drenched street at night, splashing in puddles, overjoyed at being in love. That unforgettable scene inspired this charming arrangement.

A child's red-and-black umbrella sets the color scheme, executed with red gerberas with black centers. Appropriately named umbrella plants tower over the other components. Rain is communicated with bear grass, bundled and wedged around the edge of the container. Fountains at Filoli join the chorus.

Botanical Whimsy
Maryjo Garre

> *A Boat Afloat, Becalmed on a Sea of Boxwood.*
> *Dog Chases Man Through Field of Heather.*
> *Alien Allium Captures Ginger Man; Dog Escapes.*

Supply your own headline for this whimsical arrangement, below, composed of Egyptian onions rising from allium blossoms and scampered over by a "boy and dog"—knobs of ginger root. Hyacinth sticks, inserted into the ginger and the hollow stems of the onions, are impaled on *kenzans* (pin holders) to keep the components upright. The composition rests on a boxwood parterre in the Chicago Botanic Garden.

Guardian of the Garden
Arabella S. Dane

A collaboration between the arranger and a metal arts instructor resulted in this imaginative rendition of a praying mantis. Well armed, prepared to hold off all invaders and eat all pesky insects, she struts through the garden as if she owns it. A broken saw blade serves as her forearm, ancient pliers her mouth, and a car spring the thorax. Artfully poised on one leg, she sways, just a bit, to let you know she's alive.

    The mantis has picked a bouquet of hot-colored flowers and fruit— pincushion protea, calla lilies, gerberas, glads, orchids, lemons, peppers. They're all tucked into an Oasis bouquet holder. She leans on her shovel, an inverted heliconia, as she stops to smell the flowers.

STUDY IN BAMBOO
Anne Crumpacker

This bamboo sculpture—a study in geometric shapes, planes, and space—can be moved around a Portland, Oregon, garden, calling attention to the treasures at every turn. First on the stone terrace, mortared with moss, it points to a tiny pink azalea, sweet woodruff, and ajuga bordering a path into clipped box hedges. On the edge of the lawn, catching the dappled light, it rests beside a rhododendron that has carpeted the garden floor with white blossoms. And, by the reflecting pool, its form is mirrored, as are the colors of the azaleas and rhododendrons in the background.

The artist was drawn to bamboo as a sculptural medium because of its natural beauty, its utilitarian quality, and its spiritual symbolism. She explains, "For thousands of years, bamboo—a hollow grass, the fastest-growing plant on earth—has been one of the single most important and useful plants to the largest number of people in the world. It has found its way into folklore, rituals, sports, construction, the arts and music, the kitchen, and the garden.

"In Asian cultures, bamboo is a symbol of strength, flexibility, tenacity, endurance, compromise, adaptability, virtue, honesty, longevity, loyalty, and friendship, even in adversity. For all of these reasons and more, it is beautiful to work with."

FLOWER-FREE DESIGNS
The art of flower arranging cultivates an appreciation for all plant material, not just the flowers. Any natural material—branches, roots, vines, stems, or stalks—will serve a design purpose. The Sogetsu school of ikebana has led the way in innovative abstract and minimalist designs, often with no flowers.

Wait a minute. No flowers? If there are no flowers, should these be called flower arrangements? Some would argue not, that a line should be drawn somewhere and it should be on the side of flowers. On the far side of that line, let there be another category, possibly botanic sculpture but not *flower arranging*.

But flowerless designs have an advantage. They can sharpen our awareness of the natural world, opening our eyes to form, pattern, texture, even color in a way that flowers cannot. Flowers, with their high impact, luscious texture, and brilliant color, tend to steal the show. In an arrangement with flowers, we are less likely to contemplate the texture or pattern of the secondary components because our eye is drawn to and dwells on the showier blossoms. Without that distraction—in a flower-free arrangement—we have the opportunity to appreciate more fully the subtleties of the material—the surface texture of an aged piece of wood, the spaces enclosed by bare branches, the changing light on a bamboo construction.

On this and the following pages, flowerless arrangements in the ikebana style are placed in garden settings. Here they can be admired not only for their own qualities but for how they highlight features in the garden. They make us pause a little longer, look a little closer.

PUNCTUATION
Gail Emmons

Loops of bear grass, massed in the Sogetsu manner, echo the rounded
mounds of herbs. A bleached, weathered piece of wood found in
the Oregon Cascades rises on point and leads the eye back to silver
artemisia in the knot garden at Filoli in Woodside, California. This spec-
tacularly beautiful garden is made even more interesting with this piece
of botanic sculpture.

TREES AND SHADOWS
Gail Emmons

In this sculpture, opposite, the black pieces are as vertical as the
clipped yew alleé behind them; the red branches cross their paths and
follow the lengthening evening shadows. Exemplifying true natural
balance, the placement of the red branches—which are inserted
through the black verticals—varies each time the piece is set up,
depending on the lay of the land. The branches are from a hedge of
twenty-five pittosporum, removed years ago and saved. The alleé
contains some of the two hundred Irish yews at Filoli.

APPENDICES

FLOWER ARRANGING—A CONTINUING JOURNEY

Flower arranging is an ever-changing and evolving art form that offers an opportunity for creativity and self-expression at every level—novice, experienced, professional. But just as the stone sculptor needs a good chisel and the portrait artist a fine brush, just as the cook benefits from a good recipe, and as one artist is inspired by the work of another, the flower arranger needs appropriate equipment, contact with peers, and sound information. With resources, the arranger is able to transform a creative vision into a work of art. In the accumulated information and enthusiasm of arrangers with decades of experience, here are the tools and contacts to continue a journey along the path of flower arranging.

appendix A   The Flower Arranging Study Group— Spreading the Word, Sharing the Enthusiasm

THE INFORMATION in this section has been compiled by members of the Flower Arranging Study Group of the Garden Club of America. What is the Study Group? In the words of chair Ruth Crocker, "It is a teaching arm of the Garden Club of America; its aims closely parallel those of the parent organization. The Flower Arranging Study Group is committed to increasing the knowledge and love of flower arranging, to sharing the advantages of association by means of educational workshops, correspondence, and publications, and to enhancing and protecting the beauty of the environment through the creativity of flower arranging." She recalls the beginning of the organization and describes its ongoing functions:

"In the 1970s and 1980s, flower arranging as an art form was gaining a following in the United States, but there was limited opportunity for an exchange of ideas and methods. In 1990, to fill this gap, a small but ardent band of garden club members formed the Flower Arranging Study Group to offer educational opportunities and provide exposure to international trends. A newsletter, workshops, and participation in world flower shows would be the means to these ends."

The newsletter was an immediate success. Published quarterly, it contains a calendar of worldwide flower-arranging events, articles on subjects from the practical to the theoretical, and full-color photographs of outstanding arrangements from flower shows across the country and abroad. Now titled *GCA By Design*, it is available by subscription.

Featuring teachers of international fame, the workshops have been sell-outs.

Originally planned for one group of students, the Study Group workshops are now back-to-back two-day sessions with thirty students in each of two groups. Instructors have included Althea Higham and Charles Kinnear of South Africa, Henk Mulder of Holland, Olga Meneur and Monique Gautier of France, Gregor Lersh of Germany, and Loly Marsano, Gin Rebaudi, and Carla Barbaglia of Italy. The visiting instructors frequently continue their teaching tour by giving demonstrations and workshops to garden clubs and botanical gardens across the country. The students return home to share the new styles with other flower arrangers.

The third element of the Flower Arranging Study Group's effort—besides the newsletter and workshops—is participation in international flower shows. In 1996 GCA's Flower Arranging Study Group was elected to membership in the World Association of Flower Arrangers (WAFA), representing the United States. Lucinda Seale, former liaison from the Study Group to WAFA, explains the international body this way:

"The World Association of Flower Arrangers is made up of organizations of amateur flower arrangers around the world, each representing its country. Currently there are twenty-seven member countries. Founded in 1981, WAFA meetings and flower shows are held every three years and have been hosted by England, Belgium, France, Canada, New Zealand, and South Africa. Glasgow, Scotland, was the site of the 2002 show, which had thirty-six design classes with twenty exhibitors in each class—more than seven hundred flower arrangements. The 2005 show will be in Japan."

Top, plant materials have been conditioned and wait in pails to be distributed to the thirty workshop participants. During the two-day session, four containers will be filled with sunflowers and onions, anthuriums and irises, nerines, chrysanthemums, and mushrooms.

Each participant receives the same combination of material. A visiting instructor, in this case Carla Barbaglia of Italy, demonstrates different designs—freestyle, layered, modern mass, mass and space—and encourages the students to attempt their own version with the material at hand.

Above, each arranger received fifteen sunflowers, six stalks of blue delphinium, ten blue iris blossoms, and assorted leaves. Barbaglia demonstrated the modern mass style with other kinds of plant material, teaching the principles of the style while encouraging participants not to copy but to exercise their own creative vision.

Just five rules governed the entries:

- An exhibit is made of plant material, with or without accessories, within a space specified in the show schedule.
- Plant material must predominate over all other components of the exhibit.
- The use of artificial plant material is forbidden unless stated in the regulations.
- Fresh plant material must be in water or in water-retaining material unless such material will remain turgid throughout the event.
- Painted and/or artificially colored plant material may be used unless otherwise stated in the regulations.

The opportunity to compete and judge on the international level broadens horizons and stimulates arrangers to perform at the highest level of this art. Their talent and efforts are appreciated; public attendance at the shows usually tops 25,000.

Below, five of the workshop participants show what can be done with a large silvered ceramic container, ten onions, twenty aspidistra leaves, fifteen stems of white stock, and five pieces of eucalyptus bark. The results are all successful and all different, testimony to a teacher who challenges the most experienced arranger and convinces the novice that any-thing is possible.

TRAVELING WITH PLANT MATERIAL

How can arrangers, gardeners, and other travelers carry plant material out of one country and into another—without the material being confiscated and destroyed at customs? The answer is a Phytosanitary Certificate.

To carry plant material from the United States into a foreign country, you will need an International Federal Phytosanitary Certificate (FPC) for each type of plant material you are exporting with you.

The intended purpose of the FPC is to expedite the entry of domestic plants or plant products into a foreign country. The issuing agency—in America, the United States Department of Agriculture (USDA)—certifies to the foreign plant-protection service that the shipment has been inspected and was found to conform to the phytosanitary import requirements of that country.

To find your local office of the USDA, phone 202-720-2791. You must make an appointment, and then you and your plant material must travel to that local office for inspection not more than fourteen days before your departure. Botanical names will be required. A certificate in English will be issued for which you will pay a modest fee. The certificate states that the plant material has been officially inspected in the country of origin, complies with statutory requirements for entry into the designated foreign country, is free from quarantine pests and diseases, and is substantially free from other organisms. Don't leave home without it!

When exhibiting in flower shows outside the United States, the host country will provide a list of certain plant material—with Latin and common names, and countries of origin—which are prohibited entry under any circumstances. For example, *Tsuga*, i.e., hemlock, may not enter Northern Ireland from any non-European country.

To bring plant material back into the United States, check with the United States Department of Agriculture at the number above for specific requirements. It's not easy but it is possible to travel with flowers.

appendix B   Conditioning—The Power of Flower Care

FRESH, CRISP flowers lift our spirits, but the drooped head of a rose or the wilted petals of a lily are sad sights indeed. While part of the magic of flowers is their ephemeral quality, we want to enjoy them in their pristine condition as long as possible. Conditioning —the care flowers are given as soon as they reach your hands, either from the garden or the market—can make all the difference. Pauline Runkle has had her own floral design business for thirty years, and her day-in, day-out experience with every kind of flower, under every kind of circumstance—from heat waves to snow storms—has taught her valuable lessons about the care and treatment of plant material. The wisdom that follows is based on Runkle's years of trial and error, trial and success.

WATER, WATER, WATER

More than 90 percent of the weight of most plant tissue is made up of water. Every step you take in conditioning plant material, therefore, is aimed at facilitating the uptake of water. When the plant was growing, it absorbed water from its roots and from the atmosphere. We want the blossom to continue that process as much as possible after it has been severed from the mother plant. This requires forethought and preparation on the arranger's part.

The adjustment from living, growing blossom to stable, conditioned cut flower takes planning. If you intend to work on your arrangement on Wednesday using flowers from your garden, take a preliminary walk on Monday, noting what's blooming and deciding on possible combinations. Tuesday morning, set out early with a pail you have sterilized with a rinse of chlorine-based bleach. (Runkle washes out her five-gallon pails with running water, a splash [about an eighth of a cup] of bleach, and a toilet brush with artificial bristles—natural bristles dissolve in the bleach.) Fill your pail at least half full with either hot or warm fresh water. Add the manufacturer's recommended amount of floral preservative for the quantity of water.

Let's review the cautions in the preceding paragraph—beyond using a spotlessly clean pail:

1. The first is the time of day: *Early morning and evening are the only times of day to successfully cut flowers from the garden.* During the heat of the day, the water and sugar levels in flowers are low so you will be starting with already depleted blossoms.

2. The second word to the wise is that the pail should be at least half full. (If this makes the pail too heavy to carry, consider a small cart.) Flowers absorb water through the entire length of their stems. Putting flowers in only an inch or two of water is a missed opportunity at the beginning of the conditioning process.

3. The third lesson to note is the temperature of the water. Woody-stemmed flowers—hydrangeas, roses—and branches such as dogwood and lilacs benefit from hot water. Most other flowers do well in warm water. The warmer temperature expands the cells that take up water; cold or icy water contracts those cells.

4. Fourth, floral preservative is important but equally important is the correct amount of it—what the manufacturer recommends. Dr. Michael S. Reid, writing in the summer 2000 newsletter of the California Ornamental Research Federation, summarized the effects of floral preservatives. "Cut flowers placed in fresh flower foods," Reid reported, "can remain decorative for at least twice as long as those in water alone. . . . They extend flower longevity by providing three essential ingredients—a biocide, sugar, and an acidifier." The biocide kills bacteria, yeast, and fungi in the water and on the stems. "When cut flower stems are placed in water," Reid explains, "the microbes that are present grow rapidly, feeding on the sap that bleeds from the cut stem. It has been shown that within a day of placing a freshly-cut rose stem in a clean vase containing tap water, nearly thirty million bacteria may be present in each ounce of vase water." Sugar, the second component, is the flower's food supply for completing development, bud opening, and maintaining color. The third ingredient, an acidifying agent, enables the water to move up the stem more easily. Following the manufacturer's recommendation on amounts is key because too high a concentration of the biocide will injure the flowers as well as kill the microbes, and too much sugar will cause leaf burn.

5. The fifth point to consider is timing. After being cut Tuesday morning, your blossoms and branches will have all day Tuesday and Tuesday night to "harden," that is, to take in water and adjust to having been severed from the parent plant. They will do this best in a cool, dark area—a garage, basement, or designated "flower room." The coolness and the lack of light slow the processes that were under way—the plant moving through the blooming stage to producing seeds for reproduction.

A CLEAN CUT

Cut stems with a very sharp knife or with bypass clippers. This clean cut leaves cells open to the absorption of water. Dull clippers crush the stems and limit the uptake. To reduce the spread of plant viruses, it is a good idea to dip your clippers or knife in alcohol or bleach before setting out to the garden. Scrubbing the clippers with a Teflon pad cleans off accumulated sap and allows them to do a better cutting job.

You have already determined on Monday what you are likely to cut on Tuesday, but look again. If critters have nibbled the leaves or flowers, or if the neighbor's dog—or yours—has bruised or broken your choice blossoms so they are no longer things of beauty, pass them by. They will not improve with cutting, conditioning, and being placed in an arrangement.

The new leaves of spring, on trees and shrubs and emerging from the ground, almost glow with translucent freshness, and the temptation to cut is great. Before you clip, however, be aware that these tender shoots will challenge even the best conditioning procedures. Some plant material, particularly young hosta leaves and newly opened hydrangea blossoms, are like fragile newborns and need time to gain strength and firm up before cutting.

WHAT'S THE ANGLE?

Cut stems at a 45-degree angle. This will give them the largest surface area with which to draw up water. Those woody-stemmed flowers and branches we mentioned earlier—hydrangeas and roses, dogwoods and lilacs, as well as chrysanthemums—should be cut at a 45-degree angle, then cut vertically, up the stem several times, to a distance of one to two inches. This provides more surface exposure for the uptake of water. You need really sharp clippers for this.

Flower folklore used to recommend crushing the stems of certain branches—pounding them with a hammer or even driving your car over the stems! Runkle has said that recent science advises against this practice as it destroys columns of cells in the woody, outside tissue—the "pipeline" for delivering water up to the flower.

Where you cut is also important for some flowers. Look closely at carnations, phlox, and baby's breath. Along the stem you will notice enlarged protruding areas known as nodes. The nodes don't take in water very well so cut at a 45-degree angle above or between nodes for maximum absorption.

WHICH LEAVES TO LEAVE

Foliage that will be under water in the half-full pail should be removed. Leaves under water decay rapidly and add bacteria to conditioning water. The slimy quality of the decaying material is certainly unappealing, but, more important, the bacteria the leaves produce work to close the stem end of flowers, cutting off their absorption of fluid. This does not mean you should remove all leaves, just the ones at or below water level. Leaves near the blossom act as a siphon, drawing water up the stem.

While you're removing leaves that will be below water level, you might also remove all the thorns on roses. Left on, they will punish you later by pricking fingers and tangling with other material as you work on your arrangement. With a good pair of gardening gloves, snap off each thorn. Don't use rose strippers; these tools rip the fiber and weaken the stem, exposing it to bacteria.

LIKE FLOWERS FLOCK TOGETHER

Once you've cut your plant material, sort it so that like materials are in the same bucket—lilies with lilies, roses with roses, and so forth. Some material is quite insistent on this separation. Euphorbia and narcissi, for example, exude a toxic sap that can contaminate the water and wreak havoc on their neighbors if placed in the same pail. Later they can be combined in an arrangement quite happily, but in the conditioning phase they definitely need their space and isolation.

A SEARING QUESTION

Euphorbias—poinsettias, spurge, snow-on-the-mountain, crown-of-thorns—require additional special treatment. The cut stems of these plants exude a sticky, white sap. This outward flow is a visible loss of their vital fluids and makes the intake of water impossible. Two treatments, scalding and searing, can help alleviate this problem. Experiment with a piece of your particular plant material to see how it responds.

The scalding method suggests holding the cut stems in boiling water—while protecting the blossoms from heat—for two or three minutes. The burning method involves holding the cut stem of a poinsettia, for example, over a candle flame for thirty seconds. This chars the end of the stem, stops the loss of sap, and permits the uptake of water. This usually works and is a great way to use the poinsettia blossoms that remain in late winter after the plant has lost its holiday exuberance. (Alternately, you can also buy poinsettias in the size you need for your arrangement, remove them from their pots, discard some of the soil, and tuck the roots and a bit of the damp soil into a plastic bag, securing the bag around the stem with a twist-tie. The whole can then be wired or taped to stakes and inserted into an arrangement.)

Poppies also require the cauterizing treatment, and any number of other plants respond favorably to it. These include forget-me-not, anemone, baptisia, balloon flower, Canterbury bells, clematis, columbine, coral bells, celosia, dahlia, digitalis, peony, penstemon, verbascum, Michaelmas daisy, hollyhock, primula, ranunculus, and trollius. Queen Ann's lace seems to do best when put in a pail with two inches of hot water. When the water has cooled, fill the pail to half full and add preservative. (See *Recommended Reading* for books and booklets that deal with specific varieties.)

The large, woody stems of rhododendron behave better if cut at a 45-degree angle, then slit up the stem for an inch or two, then held over a flame for three to five minutes. Plunge into deep water and leave overnight.

Flowers with hollow stems—amaryllis, delphinium, and lupine—are able to take up water inside and out. Runkle inverts the flower, pours water into the stem, plugs it with cotton, wraps the stem with elastic to keep it from splitting, then places the stem in deep water.

SUBMERSION MAY BE THE ONLY ANSWER

The broad surfaces of hosta, bergenia, cabbage and galax leaves, strands of ivy, and even some hydrangea heads benefit from being fully submerged in tepid water for an hour, then removed and left to condition in pails of water overnight. Galax, ivy, and cabbage can be put in plastic bags as soon as removed from the bath and refrigerated. The first two, galax and ivy, will keep for weeks this way.

Conifers—pine, spruce, and so forth—appreciate an hour's soak. Afterward, slit the stems and place in water up to the first needled branch.

Having traveled from Hawaii or the Caribbean out of water, tropicals—anthurium, heliconia, ginger, bird of paradise—welcome being immersed for a few minutes to an hour. (A bathtub is a good shape and size for the tall stems.) After removal, cut the stems and condition in a pail of water. These blossoms will then last a long time in your arrangement, even if your design requires them to be out of water, i.e., upside down.

Proteas, while exotic, are not tropicals and prefer cool storage temperatures, even down to 40 degrees. Runkle recommends using floral food, placing in a well-lit area, and being sure to remove leaves below water level. All these steps help prevent black spots on the leaves.

Some plant material requires a particularly high level of humidity. When you buy maidenhair fern and mimosa, the delicate leaves and blossoms are sealed in plastic bags. Leave them there and refrigerate the bags until you're ready to arrange.

BUYER BEWARE

When you are cutting in your garden, you know that the "gone-by" daisy is not going to get a second life once you cut it and bring it inside. The "gone-by" flowers at the florist, corner market, or grocery store are not going to rejuvenate miraculously either. There are a lot of unknown variables in the life of commercial flowers—when they were harvested in South America, California, or Holland; when they arrived at the wholesaler; when the retailer received them; how or if they were conditioned; how long they have been sitting on the floor or in the cooler. Look them over carefully. If the blossoms look transparent, thinning around the edges, they're probably old. Lift the flowers out of the bucket and check the stems. If the leaves have turned yellow or the stems are slimy, they are past their prime. No amount of careful conditioning will breathe life back into them.

Once home, treat your market flowers the way you treat your garden flowers—cut off an inch or more of the stem and place them in clean pails half full of water with the proper amount of floral preservative added. Allow them to rest and resuscitate in a cool, dark place overnight, or at least for a few hours.

A GOOD NIGHT'S REST

Having carefully prepared your plant material for its overnight conditioning, where do you leave those pails? We suggest the garage, basement, or flower room, all good possibilities unless—unless there is ethylene gas. This odorless gas causes the premature aging of plants, resulting in buds falling off and leaves turning yellow. Freesias, alstroemerias, carnations, and roses are particularly susceptible. Ethylene gas comes from decaying garbage, ripening fruit, fungi, and exhaust fumes. Storing a basket of ripening fruit next to the flowers you plan to use in your flower-and-fruit arrangement can hasten the flowers' demise. Separate them until the moment of arranging.

Watch the temperature in your storage area. You want cool but not freezing. If the water in the cells of the flower freezes, the cells burst, damaging the flowers and foliage. When flowers are kept cool, at about 38–50 degrees, they stay stable and the aging process is slowed.

INTENSIVE CARE

Some flowers, such as tulips and gerberas, may arrive limp from shipping, even though they are fresh. If so, wrap newspaper around the bunch to hold the blossoms upright, secure with a rubber band or string, recut the ends of the stems, and immerse in a bucket of water up to the flower head. If there is a white part at the base of the stem of a tulip or hyacinth, be sure to cut above it. This portion does not absorb water well.

Pricking the stems of tulips, irises, and hellebores just under the flower head helps to release air blocks, allowing water to travel up to the blossom.

Be particularly careful about purchasing lilies. There are different grades of these flowers, and what may seem like a wonderful bargain in price may turn out to be a disappointment in performance. The stems should be strong enough to proudly hold up the flowers if you plan to use them in a tall arrangement. If, instead, you can use short stems in tight centerpieces, you may be able to take advantage of the bargains.

Lilies, including the marvelous white Casa Blancas, often come in tight bud. Buy early and condition them in a warmer place to encourage the flowers to open.

Removing the brown, pollen-bearing anthers from lilies can prolong their vase life and prevent staining disasters. If pollen falls on the flower itself, blot it with a cotton ball; do not rub or use water. If the pollen gets onto clothing, touch it with a piece of masking or Scotch tape. This acts as a magnet, pulling off the pollen grains.

THE KINDEST CUT OF ALL

There is great debate concerning the necessity and/or success of cutting under water, a practice that is followed religiously by ikebana arrangers. The retail florist trade seems to be convinced of its merit, and has developed specialized equipment—a trough of water into which the stems are placed to be recut by a guillotinelike blade. Cutting under water, the argument goes, prevents air from entering the stem and blocking the uptake of water.

Runkle, too, says she's convinced. In the garden, when she cuts a stem from a plant and places it in the pail, she dips her clippers into the water and makes a fresh cut about an inch up the stem. If a flower in an arrangement wilts, she removes that stem and fills a clean container with almost-hot water. She puts clippers and stem under water and makes a fresh cut an inch up from the bottom of the stem, then leaves the stem in the hot water and watches while the flower draws it up. Roses with bent heads and wilted hydrangea blossoms respond to this treatment. Fully submerging them in warm or tepid water for an hour works, too.

EQUAL TIME

Don't neglect yourself while you're taking care of your plant material. If you are working with alstroemeria, resist pinching off leaves with your fingernails. These flowers carry a fungus in their sap that can get trapped under the nail and cause problems. Many com-

- **"Grind down the welds"**: refers to cleaning up the welded seams or joints by grinding off the extra metal. This makes the structure look professionally made.
- **Cost**: Get a written estimate for the work.
- **Backup**: Keep a second copy of your drawing at home.

When you have gone to the trouble of making a piece, or having one built, spend the extra money to have it sand-blasted and professionally painted. In your jeans-and-sweat-shirt uniform, take your new creation to a shop that paints cars, terrace furniture, and other metal objects. The range of colors will thrill you, the finish will have wonderful depth, and it will last for years.

If your construction is going to be hidden by plant material, prime and paint it yourself. You can take a friend out to lunch with the money you save.

appendix D   Flower Shows—Dates and Locations

INSPIRATION and fresh concepts are the treasured currency of all artists. For flower arrangers the best place to look for the elusive muse is at top-quality flower shows. There the visitor will find the latest fashions in the handling of plant material; a never-before-seen blossom that has just entered the world market; a container that would be perfect in a spot at home; an ingenious method of elevating a design. We heartily recommend the following major flower shows, which are held regularly in the locations given. Eight are sponsored by Garden Club of America clubs; the others are sponsored by botanical gardens and horticultural societies and offer GCA awards. Exact dates may be obtained via the telephone number provided.

MAJOR FLOWER SHOWS

CALIFORNIA, Oakland
Oakland Museum of California
1000 Oak Street
Oakland, CA 94607
510-238-2200 (museum director)
"Visions," sponsored by five Bay Area clubs: Carmel-by-the-Sea Garden Club, Hillsborough Garden Club, Orinda Garden Club, Piedmont Garden Club, and Woodside-Atherton Garden Club; in April, 2005, then every three years.

CONNECTICUT, Greenwich
Christ Church
254 East Putnam Avenue
Greenwich, CT 06830
203-869-6600
"Preview of Spring," sponsored by Green Fingers Garden Club; in March, odd-numbered years.

GEORGIA, Atlanta
Atlanta Exposition Center North
3650 Jonesboro Road SE
Atlanta, GA 30354
404-888-5638
Southeastern Flower Show, sponsored by Atlanta Botanical Garden; in February, annually.

HAWAII, Honolulu
Honolulu Academy of Arts
900 S. Beretania Street
Honolulu, HI 96814
808-532-8700
Title varies; sponsored by Garden Club of Honolulu; in April, 2003, then every three years.

ILLINOIS, Chicago
Chicago Horticultural Society Botanic Garden
1000 Lake Cook Road
Glencoe, IL 60022
847-835-5440
"Show of Summer," sponsored by six area garden clubs: Garden Club of Barrington, Garden Club of Evanston, Garden Guild of Winnetka, Kenilworth Garden Club, Lake Forest Garden Club, and Winnetka Garden Club; in June, even-numbered years.

MASSACHUSETTS, Boston
Bayside Exposition and Conference Center
200 Mount Vernon Street
Boston, MA 02125
617-474-6000
New England Spring Flower Show, sponsored by the Massachusetts Horticultural Society; in March, annually.

OHIO, Cleveland
Cleveland Botanical Garden
11030 East Boulevard
Cleveland, OH 44106
216-721-1600 x176
Cleveland Botanical Garden Flower Show, sponsored by the Cleveland Botanical Garden; in May/June, even-numbered years.

OREGON, Portland
Portland Art Museum
1219 SW Park Avenue
Portland, OR 97205
503-226-2811
"Inspirations...," sponsored by Portland Garden Club; April 30/May 1, 2004, then every three years.

PENNSYLVANIA, Philadelphia
Pennsylvania Convention Center
12th and Arch Streets
Philadelphia, PA 19106
215-988-8800
The Philadelphia Flower Show, sponsored by the Pennsylvania Horticultural Society; in March, annually.

TENNESSEE, Memphis
Dixon Gallery and Gardens
4339 Park Avenue
Memphis, TN 38117
901-761-2409 (gallery)
Title varies, sponsored by Memphis Garden Club; in April, even-numbered years.

TEXAS, Houston
Museum of Fine Arts, Houston
1001 Bissonnet at Main
Houston, TX 77005
713-639-7300
"Florescence," sponsored by the Garden Club of Houston, River Oaks Garden Club, and the Museum of Fine Arts, Houston; in April, odd-numbered years.

WISCONSIN, Milwaukee
Milwaukee Art Museum
700 N. Art Museum Drive
Milwaukee, WI 53202
414-224-3220
"Art en Fleurs," sponsored by four area garden clubs: Green Tree Garden Club, Kettle Moraine Garden Club, Lake Geneva Garden Club, and Town and Country Garden Club; in August 2004, then every three years.

MUSEUM FLOWER SHOWS
The following art museums and galleries host flower festivals or judged flower shows on a regular basis. These events draw thousands of visitors to view the relationship between the museums' works of art and the interpretive floral art that the arrangers contribute. To determine the exact date of an event, call or write the museum at the address given.

ALABAMA, Birmingham
Birmingham Museum of Art
2000 Eighth Avenue North
Birmingham, AL 35203
205-254-2707
"Art in Bloom"; March, even-numbered years.

CALIFORNIA, Oakland
Oakland Museum of California
1000 Oak Street
Oakland, CA 94607
510-238-2200
"Visions"; April 2005, then every three years.

CALIFORNIA, San Diego
San Diego Museum of Art
1450 El Prado, Balboa Park, P.O. Box 122107
San Diego, CA 92112
619-232-7931
"Art Alive"; May, annually.

CALIFORNIA, San Francisco
California Palace of the Legion of Honor
100 34th Avenue, Lincoln Park
San Francisco, CA 94121
415-750-3504
"Bouquets to Art"; March, annually.

CONNECTICUT, Hartford
The Wadsworth Atheneum
600 Main Street
Hartford, CT 06103
860-278-2670 x3141
"Festival of Fine Art and Flowers";
March/April, annually.

DELAWARE, Wilmington
Delaware Art Museum
2301 Kentmere Parkway
Wilmington, DE 19806
302-571-9590, x569
"Art in Bloom"; April, even-numbered years.

GEORGIA, Athens
University of Georgia,
Georgia Museum of Art
90 Carlton Street
Athens, GA 30602
706-542-0451
"Gardens to Galleries"; March, irregular timetable.

HAWAII, Honolulu
Honolulu Academy of Arts
900 S. Beretania Street
Honolulu, HI 96814
808-532-8700
Title varies; April 2003, then every three years.

LOUISIANA, Monroe
Biedenharn Museum and Gardens
(ELsong Gardens)
2006 Riverside Drive
Monroe, LA 71201
318-387-5281
Title varies; spring, odd-numbered years.

LOUISIANA, New Orleans
New Orleans Museum of Art
P.O. Box 19123
One Collins C. Diboll Circle
New Orleans, LA 70179
504-483-2316
"Art in Bloom"; March, annually.

MARYLAND, Baltimore
The Walters Art Gallery
600 N. Charles Street
Baltimore, MD 21201
410-547-9000, x277
"Art Blooms at The Walters"; spring, annually.

MASSACHUSETTS, Boston
Museum of Fine Arts, Boston
Avenue of the Arts, 465 Huntington Avenue
Boston, MA 02115
617-267-9300
"Art in Bloom"; April, annually since 1976.

MINNESOTA, Minneapolis
Minneapolis Institute of Arts
2400 Third Avenue South
Minneapolis, MN 55404
612-870-3131
"Art in Bloom"; May, annually.

MISSOURI, St. Louis
Saint Louis Art Museum
Fourth Park and One Fine Arts Drive
St. Louis, MO 63110
314-721-0072
"Art in Bloom"; March/April, annually.

NEW JERSEY, Trenton
New Jersey State Museum
205 W. State Street
Trenton, NJ 08625
609-394-5310
Title varies; November, irregular timetable.

NEW MEXICO, Santa Fe
Gerald Peters Gallery
1011 Paseo de Peralta
Santa Fe, NM 87501
505-955-0701
"Milagro de las Flores"; June, irregular timetable.

NEW YORK, Garrison
Desmond Fish Library
P. O. Box 265
Garrison, NY 10524
845-424-3020
Title varies; September, odd-numbered years.

NEW YORK, Rochester
University of Rochester Memorial
Art Gallery
500 University Avenue
Rochester, NY 14607
716-473-7720
"Art in Bloom"; April, even-numbered years.

OHIO, Akron
Akron Art Museum
70 E. Market Street
Akron, OH 44308
330-376-9185
"Art Blooms!"; irregular timetable.

OREGON, Portland
Portland Art Museum
1219 S.W. Park Avenue
Portland, OR 97205
503-226-2811
"Inspirations..."; April 30/May 1, 2004,
then every three years.

PENNSYLVANIA, Philadelphia
University of Pennsylvania Museum of
Archaeology and Anthropology
33rd and Spruce Streets
Philadelphia, PA 19104
215-898-9202
"Artifacts in Bloom"; January, even-numbered years.

RHODE ISLAND, Newport
Newport Art Museum
76 Bellevue Avenue
Newport, RI 02840
401-848-8200
Title varies; fall, annually.

RHODE ISLAND, Newport
Rosecliff Mansion
424 Bellevue Avenue
Newport, RI 02840
401-847-1000
"The Newport Flower Show"; July, annually.

TENNESSEE, Memphis
Dixon Gallery and Gardens
4339 Park Avenue
Memphis, TN 38117
901-761-2409
Title varies; April, even-numbered years.

TENNESSEE, Nashville
Cheekwood Botanical Garden and
Museum of Art
1800 Forest Park Drive
Nashville, TN 37205
615-356-8000
Title varies; October 2003, every three years.

TEXAS, Beaumont
Art Museum of Southeast Texas
500 Main Street
Beaumont, TX 77701
409-832-3432
"Magnolia in Bloom"; October, odd-numbered years.

TEXAS, Houston
Museum of Fine Arts, Houston
1001 Bissonnet at Main
Houston, TX 77005
713-639-7300
"Florescence"; April, odd-numbered years.

VIRGINIA, Norfolk
The Chrysler Museum of Art
245 W. Olney Road
Norfolk, VA 23510
757-664-6200
"Flowers and Art"; spring, irregular timetable.

VIRGINIA, Richmond
Virginia Museum of Fine Arts
2800 Grove Avenue at The Boulevard
Richmond, VA 23221
804-340-1400
"Fine Arts and Flowers"; October, odd-numbered
years.

WISCONSIN, Milwaukee
Milwaukee Art Museum
700 N. Art Museum Drive
Milwaukee, WI 53202
414-224-3220
"Art en Fleurs"; August 2004; every three years.

INTERNATIONAL FLOWER SHOWS
Most countries host flower shows, many on an
annual basis. Dates and locations of shows around
the world appear in flower-arranging periodicals,
including *GCA By Design*.

appendix E Sources and Resources for the Flower Arranger

SOURCES FOR FLOWER-ARRANGING SUPPLIES

Flower arrangers are known for their eagle eyes and highly developed skill in acquiring components in unlikely places. Dumps, discount stores, and antique and junk shops are potential sources for containers and bases. Any curbside pile of storm debris could yield a gem—a curved branch, a twisted vine, a palm spaeth, some catalpa pods—as could many a mile of roadside. The occasional unauthorized, albeit judicious "pruning" of an overhanging branch has led to the saying that all you need to be a flower arranger is a sharp pair of clippers and a fast car.

While these sources are certainly valuable, the arranger will at times need more predictable ones. Urban centers offer kenzans (pin holders) in a wide range of sizes, containers of varied descriptions, and the latest in fresh and dried flowers from around the world, but not every community can boast the same selection. Flower arrangers have found the following to be valuable sources for interesting containers, flower-arranging equipment, fresh and dried flowers.

Note that some firms are 'wholesale only.' In order to purchase directly from a wholesale supplier, a buyer must have a federal employer ID number and a state resale tax number certificate. Your florist might use the following information to locate the material you need and order it for you. Lead time for the unusual or for large quantities should be two to three weeks.

CONTAINERS AND OTHER FLOWER-ARRANGING EQUIPMENT

Rockport Pottery
140 Vinal Road
Rockport, ME 04856
207-236-8923
The potter-owner creates traditional ikebana containers in an array of glazes, colors, and shapes, as well as beautifully crafted one-of-a-kind containers for Western-style designs. Retail.

McTaggart's
P. O. Box 60991
Longmeadow, MA 01116
413-567-0993
Bob McTaggart represents numerous talented potters and also carries a wide range of kenzans and flower-arranging supplies. These wares can be purchased at his booth at the Philadelphia Flower Show and certain other flower shows. Call or write for his next venue. Retail.

Country House Floral Supply
P. O. Box 853
Eastham, MA 02642
508-255-6664
www.countryhousefloral.com

A popular supplier in the United States for many years, by catalog and at flower shows. One-of-a-kind and traditional ikebana containers, floral-foam cages, pin holders, wire cutters, pruners, books, gloves, and more. Retail.

Althea Higham/Flora-Mech
P. O. Box 438
Hillcrest 3650
KwaZulu-Natal, South Africa
Phone and fax: 011-27-31-767-2174
floramech@cdrive.co.za
Higham, who has conducted workshops for the Flower Arranging Study Group (see page 172), operates a specialized floral supply business with her husband. They offer a selection of kenzans, as well as equipment of their own design, including adjustable metal stands and wire-mesh Oasis cages. Send a drawing and they will customize your order. Catalog and price list available; will ship worldwide. Retail.

www.floralartmall.com
This rich New Zealand website is an online shopping mall for the flower arranger, with monthly lessons and helpful articles. For sale are books and floral art supplies—from floral foam cages, wire, and pins, to exotic stands and containers. Retail.

FRESH PLANT MATERIAL

If you're looking for a particular kind of fresh plant material or large quantities, these companies may have just what you need. Check their websites for varieties and details.

Cultivars, Inc.
P. O. Box 893
Greenwich, CT 06830
203-661-9660/866-661-9660
Fax 203-661-9663
www.cultivarsinc.com
A direct importer from Holland, Franz Joseph (F. J.) of Cultivars, Inc, will ship quality fresh materials by FedEx to both retail and wholesale customers. Visit their website to explore gift programs and more.

Florists' Review Magazine
The 'Sourcebook,' in the June issue lists wholesalers in fresh and tropical materials. See details in the Periodicals section, page 193.

flowerbuyer.com
A sophisticated website that originally provided access to three hundred flower growers in Ecuador, Colombia, Mexico, and Costa Rica and is now expanding to growers in California, Holland, Australia, and more. Buyer states quantity required and makes a bid as in a live flower auction. Bid is submitted to growers, and if there is a match, buyer is notified by e-mail. Boxed quantities. A helpful coach will walk you through a test auction; 2–3 days from ordering to shipping.

Aina Hawaiian Tropical Products
175 East Kawailani Street
Hilo, Hawaii 96720
877-961-4774
www.hawaiitropicals.com
Many varieties of fresh proteas, gingers, orchids, tropical foliage, and anthuriums—in a set number of stems per box (bulk)—may be purchased either retail or wholesale. FedEx. Wholesale minimum is $100; no minimum on retail.

Golden Land Protea
P. O. Box 301355
Escondido, CA 92030
760-751-1043

A fine short list of tropicals and protea varieties, sold by the stem. Shipped express in 1–2 days. Wholesale only; talk to your florist.

Leilani Exotics
P. O. Box 426
Pahoa, Hawaii 96778
800-889-1038
Both a grower and shipper of anthurium, including the large obake, cymbidium, and dendrobium orchids, bird of paradise, many heliconia varieties, protea, foliage, and more, including several styles of leis. Some tropicals sold in stems-per-box lots. Wholesale and retail. Will fax price list.

SOURCES FOR DRIED PLANT MATERIAL

The following companies can supply dried material in quantities that would be useful for workshops or club projects. Most are wholesale only, so your local florist might assist you in acquiring the material needed.

Coast Wholesale Florist, Inc.
149 Morris Street
San Francisco, CA 94107
415-781-3034/800-562-3681
Excellent dried and preserved flowers and foliage in a wide range— from exotic pods and cones to ostrich eggs. Sold by the bunch or bag. First order $150 minimum. Catalog available. Retail and wholesale.

Hoh Grown
P. O. Box 2083
Port Angeles, WA 98362
800-426-6677
www.hohgrown.com
Featuring mosses, fungi, lichens, driftwood, seashells, kelproots, wreaths, and garlands from the Pacific Northwest. Catalog available. Wholesale, retail on website.

Lincolnway Flower Farm
2207 Old Lincoln Highway
Lowden, IA 52255
563-941-5417
Shop by mail/phone for farm-grown dried herbs, flowers, Indian corn, gourds, and more. Dried plant materials are available year-round from stock hung inside a 100-year-old barn.

Custom work in dried wreaths, bouquets, and swags. Retail.

Schuster's of Texas, Inc.
2109 Priddy Road, Box 97
Goldthwaite, TX 76844
915-648-2267/800-351-1493
www.schustersoftexas.com
Since 1950, Schuster's has been supplying the floral trade and retailers with dried flowers, foliage, floral products, feathers, pods, and more. Catalog available for $10.00, applied against first order of $75 minimum. Retail and wholesale.

AMERICAN FLOWER MARKETS AND DISTRICTS

In the United States, there are six flower market districts where it is possible to visit wholesale vendors in close proximity to each other—Boston, New York, Los Angeles, St. Louis, San Francisco, and Portland (Oregon). Policies on purchasing vary. Some vendors sell retail; others require a business account. Even when you can't buy, a walk among the stalls or shops is a feast for the eyes and an education in what's available in the world of flowers. In Boston, New York, and Portland, the wholesalers-growers operate independently, with no central organization. Their locations are as follows:

The Boston Flower Market
500 block of Albany Street

New York City Flower District
Between Sixth and Seventh Avenues on 28th Street

Portland Flower Market District
Swann Island

The following markets have contact numbers where you may get information about hours and entry requirements.

Los Angeles Flower District Association:
American Florist Exchange
754 Wall Street
Los Angeles, CA 90014
213-622-1966

Southern California Flower Market

742 Maple Avenue (between Seventh
and Eighth Streets)
Los Angeles, CA 90014
213-627-2482
Founded in 1925, eighty growers and retailers
now participate in the largest wholesale floral
market in the U.S. Some vendors will sell retail.

LaSalle Street–St. Louis Wholesale
Flower Market

2700 block of LaSalle Street
St. Louis, MO 63104
800-826-7837
Since 1927, LaSalle Street has been home
to numerous family-owned wholesale floral
suppliers, with the first St. Louis vendors
actually opening their doors in 1890. Shortly
after the turn of the twentieth century, St.
Louis adopted the slogan "The Flower Town"
and one firm even gave away free flowers to
tourists. Today, the St. Louis Flower Market
consists of six wholesale dealers and two
retail storefront businesses.

San Francisco Flower Mart

Entrance at corner of Sixth and
Brannan Streets
San Francisco, CA 94107
415-392-7944
America's first indoor flower market was
founded in 1909 in San Francisco. Today, in its
present location, eighty-five stalls are filled
with wholesale vendors, some of whom are
also true growers. Outside the Mart gates
some vendors sell retail from storefronts;
others sell retail after the morning rush.
Call for hours.

INTERNATIONAL FLOWER MARKETS

The discussion of international flower
markets could fill its own book, but two are
clearly tourist attractions in their own right.
That at Covent Garden Market in England
is probably the oldest in the world, and the
other is certainly the world's largest, the
Aalsmeer Flower Auction in Holland.

The New Covent Garden Market–
London, England

In the thirteenth century, Benedictine monks
started the "Convent Garden," which was a
market where they could sell their surplus
garden produce. As the market grew to
become a regional horticultural market for
the city, the name became Covent Garden.
The newest Covent Garden Market, which
opened in 1974, is located in central London
on fifty-six acres at Nine Elms at Vauxhall. It
consists of two markets—the vegetable/fruit
market and the flower market. The latter is
housed in 70,000 square feet of tempera-
ture-controlled space accommodating nearly
fifty flower and plant wholesalers and ten
foliage merchants, plus various "sundries"
dealers. Plant material arrives daily from
Africa, Asia, the Caribbean, Colombia,
Denmark, Holland, Israel, Italy, and Spain.

Aalsmeer Flower Auction–
Aalsmeer, Holland

Located one hour outside Amsterdam,
Aalsmeer is visited by 170,000 tourists a year,
who may enter the Aalsmeer Flower Auction
between 7:30 A.M. and 11:00 A.M. daily.
Occupying a building the size of 125 football
fields, this largest of seven flower auctions
in the Netherlands sells seventeen million
flowers and two million plants each day, with
80 percent being exported to other countries. Plant material from growers is first
taken to a huge waiting area where it is
inspected. The buckets of cut plant material
are then loaded on large, open metal carts
and automatically moved into one of four
auction rooms. Up to 1,400 "cut buyers" bid.
After the plant material has been sold, it goes
to the distribution area, then to the buyers'
packing areas, then onto shipping pallets,
then onto waiting aircraft or refrigerated
trucks. This means that plant material sold in
the morning in Aalsmeer is ready for sale the
next morning in flower shops anywhere in
the world.

appendix F Recommended Reading

Some of the following books are current and available in bookstores; many are older editions that are still treasured by arrangers. You may be able to locate some older books through the interlibrary loan system in your state. If you're interested in purchasing out-of-print classics or foreign flower-arranging books, a list of dealers specializing in these markets appears at the end of the section.

BIBLIOGRAPHY

Aaronson, Marian. *Design with Plant Material*. London: Grower Books, 1972. This book introduced the modern art of flower arranging to many readers and it continues to instruct and inspire.

Abstracta. Genova, Italy: Luisa dePaulini–Cristina Zanobini Tormena Editore, 1996. This Italian book and the earlier *Scultura Floreale* are on the cutting edge of contemporary arranging.

Anzi, Anna, *Fantasie Floreali: L'Arte di decorare con i fiori a cura di Anna Anzi*. Genova, Italy: Mondadori, 1991. This book captures the ephemeral nature of floral art in magnificent fashion.

Arms, John Taylor, and Dorothy Noyes Arms. *Design in Flower Arrangement*. New York: Macmillan Company, 1937. This book is based on the design lectures the artist John Taylor Arms gave to garden clubs; a new insight when published and still a firm foundation for moving ahead in this art form.

Ascher, Amalie Adler. *The Complete Flower Arranger*. New York: Simon Schuster, 1974. A comprehensive textbook on flower arranging with detailed information on the elements and principles of design, containers, conditioning, and exhibiting.

Belcher, Betty. *Creative Flower Arranging: Floral Design for Home and Flower Show*. Portland, Oregon: Timber Press, 1993. Belcher followed her revision of the National Council of State Garden Club handbook with this outstanding manual on flower design.

Benz, M. Flowers: *Abstract Form II*. College Station, Texas: San Jacinto Publishing Company, 1999. This book lays out an interesting concept involving imagination, art, and communication between the artist and the viewer, using unique plant material.

Berrall, Julia S. *A History of Flower Arrangement*. New York: Viking Press, 1968. An illustrated book on the use of cut flowers from the time of the ancients to the contemporary era.

Blacker, Mary Rose. *Flora Domestica: A History of British Flower Arranging, 1500–1930*. New York: The National Trust / Harry N. Abrams, 2000. The author traces the use of flowers and plants in houses from the sixteenth century to the early twentieth.

Blacklock, Judith. *Flower Arranging Style: An International Collection of Ideas and Inspirations For All Seasons*. Boston: Bullfinch Press, 1997. A compendium of techniques, design styles, and floral fashions from around the world by this well-known British arranger and instructor.

Bridges, Derek. *Flower Arranger's Bible*. London: Cresset Press, 1985. Practical advice on every aspect of flower arranging.

Burger, Paola, and Loli Marsano. *Scultura Floreale*. Milan: Idea Book Edizioni, n.d. This book more than any other altered contemporary arranging styles. Each sculptural arrangement is accompanied by a sketch and an explanation of the design qualities at play.

Clements, Julia. *101 Ideas for Flower Arrangement*. London: C. Arthur Pearson, 1953. The teacher credited with revolutionizing flower arranging opens the doors of possibility.

Coe, Stella. *Ikebana*. New York: Overlook Press, 1984. Coe, a member of the Sogetsu school, wrote a delightful book on the basics of ikebana. She portrays ikebana as personal pleasure, bringing tranquility and fulfillment.

Cooke, Dorothy, and Pamela McNicol. *A History of Flower Arranging*. Oxford: Heinemann Professional Publishing, 1989. This publication by the National Association of Flower Arranging Societies of Great Britain is a collection of essays by various teachers, including Paola Berger and Marion Aaronson, on styles through history.

Cyphers, Emma Hodkinson. *Modern Abstract Flower Arrangements*. New York: Hearthside Press, 1964. This classic encourages the arranger to create abstract compositions from one's inner self and utilize the principles of design intuitively.

DeRudder, Marc. *Floral Masterpieces – Belgium*. Brussels, Belgium: Stichting Kunstboek Publishers, 1996. Beautifully photographed contemporary floral designs.

De Vos, Gert, Mit Ingelaere, and Eliane Joski. *Of All Flowers: 30 Years Belgian Flower Arrangement Society*. Tielt, Belgium: Uitgeverij Lannoo, 1998. Seventy teachers and demon-strators have contributed to this anthology of Belgian floral art, much of it photographed in dramatic settings.

Fazio, Rosnella Cajello, and Pereira Jenny Banti. *L'Arte dei fiori in Italia*. Milan: Leonardo-De Luca Editori, 1991. There is an inspiration on every page of this beautiful Italian book.

Flower Show and Judging Guide. New York: The Garden Club of America, 2000. This book is used by arrangers and judges in the Garden Club of America as a handbook and teaching guide.

Gautier, Monique. *Bouquets*. Paris: Editions Rustica, 1994.

———. *Bouquets exotiques*. Paris: Editions Rustica, 1997. This and the preceding book showcase the innovative designs of this outstanding French arranger.

Gibson, Cynthia. *A Botanical Touch*. New York: Viking Penquin, 1993. A watercolorist and designer of floral textiles, Gibson brings the botanical motif of the garden into every room of the home with fresh flowers, fabrics, china, linens, rugs, etc.

Gilliam, Hitomi, and John Haines. *Design Compendium – Styles and Methods*. Taiwan: World Floral Services, Inc., 1999. This book and others by Gilliam take arrangers to new levels of understanding and achievement.

Graves, Maitland. *The Art of Color and Design*. New York and London: McGraw-Hill Book Company, 1941. A basic text on the elements and principles of design as they apply to all art forms.

Guide to Period Flower Arranging. 2d ed. Leicester, England: The National Association of Flower Arrangement Societies of Great Britain, 1992. A collection of essays on period designs from early Egyptian to Art Deco. Edited by Daphne Vagg.

Hamél, Esther Veramae. *Encyclopedia of Judging and Exhibiting: Floriculture and Flora-Artistry*. 5th rev. ed. St. Ignatius, Montana: Ponderosa Publishers, 1966. The classic textbook on arranging and judging, this is probably used by more judges and arrangers in the United States than any other.

Handbook for Flower Shows. St. Louis, Missouri: National Garden Clubs, Inc., 1997. The exhibitors' and judges' manual for flower shows sponsored by National Garden Clubs, formerly National Council of State Garden Clubs.

Hannay, Frances J. *Outlines of Period Flower Arrangements*. St. Louis, Missouri: National Garden Clubs, Inc., 1991. This booklet is a primary reference for period arrangements in flower shows.

Harwell, Dan. *Searching for Design with Fibonacci and Phi*. Abilene, Texas: Golden Spiral Publishing, 1995. The golden section theory is clearly explained and illustrated in floral designs.

Hefferman, Cecelia. *Flowers A to Z: Buying, Growing, Cutting, Arranging*. New York: Harry N. Abrams, 2001. A colorful book with basic tips on tools, containers, recognizing fresh flowers, and conditioning them. Detailed photos on two dozen popular choices from agapanthus to zinnia.

Hessayon, Dr. D. G. *The Flower Arranging Expert*. London: Transworld Publishers, 1994. Advice on everything from basic mechanics to exhibiting in flower shows.

Howze, Allan, and James Moretz. *Nature Into Art—Designing With Our Planet*. Chicago: Flowerian Publishers, 1999. A contemporary guide to observing the close relationship between design in nature and design in art.

Ikenobo, Senei, Houn Ohara, and Sufu Teshigahara. *The Masters' Book of Ikebana: Background and Principles of Japanese Flower Arrangement*. Tokyo: Bijutsu Shuppansha Publishers, 1966. There is something for everyone in this book—Japanese history, art, culture, nature, plus the creative expression of ikebana, all framed by lessons from teachers of the Ikenobo, Ohara, and Sogetsu schools of ikebana.

Influences: Floral Design in New Zealand. Palmerston North, New Zealand: Floral Art Society of New Zealand, Inc., 1996. This commemorative book celebrates the hosting of the World Association of Flower Arrangers meeting in Wellington, New Zealand. It showcases the unique style and unusual plant material of the New Zealand arranger.

Ingham, Vickie L. *Elegance in Flowers—Classic Arrangements for All Seasons*. Birmingham, Alabama: Oxmoor House. A wonderful book for decorating Southern homes in the elegant "Birmingham style."

Instituto Italiano Decorazione Floreale Amatori. *Fiori Linee Strutture*. Genova, Italy: RS Editore, 2000. This gives a taste of the exciting floral art of Italy.

Johnson, James L., William J. McKinley, Jr., and M. Buddy Benz, *Flowers: Creative Design*. College Station, Texas: San Jacinto Publishing Co., 2001. This is a beautiful and valuable textbook for the amateur and professional, compiled by teachers of floral art at Texas A&M University. The eleventh printing and a complete revision of *Flowers: Geometric Form*.

Kawase, Toshiro. *Inspired Flower Arrangements*. Tokyo and New York: Kodansha International, 1990. An unusual and beautiful book of stunning photographs, bringing nature indoors with appealing style.

Komoda, Shusui, and Horst Pointner. *Ikebana Spirit and Technique*. Poole, Dorset, England: Blandford Press, 1980. A practical and technical course in ikebana that also encompasses Asian philosophy and creativity.

Kudo, Kazuhiko. *Classic Ikebana Moribana Style*. Tokyo: Shufunutomo Co., Ltd., 1996. *Moribana* means "piled up with flowers," and this book is piled up with wonderful designs.

Lersh, Gregor. *Principles of Floral Design*. Munster, Germany: Donau Verlag, 1999. The author of more than a dozen books on flower arranging, Lersh explains—with sketches and photographs—"the graphic principles of design as they contribute to the art of floristry."

Macqueen, Sheila. *Complete Flower Arranging*. London: Ward Lock, 1979. This book and others by the grand lady of English flower arranging focus on using plant materials from the garden to dramatic effect.

March-Penney, John. *Japanese Flower Arrangement/Ikebana*. London: Hamlyn Publishing Group, 1969. In eight chapters—from "How do I start?" to "How did it all begin?"—the author initiates the arranger in the history and practice of ikebana.

Marcus, Margaret Fairbanks. *Period Flower Arrangement*. New York: M. Barrows & Company, 1952. The first and still the definitive resource on period arrangements.

Moir, May A. *The Garden Watcher*. rev. ed. Honolulu: University of Hawaii, 1989. Moir's observant eye and her ability to turn the unlikely into floral art are inspirations for arrangers everywhere—not just Hawaii.

Ost, Daniel. *Leafing Through Flowers*. New York: Callaway Editions, 2000. A large format, breathtakingly beautiful book of arrangements and installations by this renowned Belgian artist.

Otis, Denise, Ronaldo Maia, and Ernst Beadle. *Decorating with Flowers*. New York: Harry N. Abrams, 1978. A beautiful book with contemporary flower designs by Maia, a master of the art. Maia followed this with *More Decorating with Flowers* in 1991.

Philpotts, Kaui. *Floral Traditions at the Honolulu Academy of Arts*. Los Angeles: Perpetua Press, 1995. An informative book on how volunteers design dramatic arrangements for the Honolulu Academy of Arts using Hawaiian plant material.

Plumb, Barbara. *A Bouquet From the Met/ Flower Arrangements by Chris Giftos at the Metropolitan Museum of Art*. New York: Harry N. Abrams, 1998. Lila Acheson Wallace's bequest to the Metropolitan Museum was "to create alive and breathing floral art," which is what Chris Giftos does for the Met and this beautiful book.

Ream, Victoria Jane. *Art in Bloom*. Salt Lake City, Utah: Deseret Equity, 1997. This book features arrangements complementing works of art. It was photographed at flower shows and Art in Bloom events in eighteen museums.

Riester, Dorothy W. *Design for Flower Arrangers*. 2d ed. New York: Van Nostrand Reinhold Company, 1971. A highly recommended text on the elements and principles of design as they apply to flower arranging.

Sato, Shozo. *The Art of Arranging Flowers: A Complete Guide to Japanese Ikebana*. New York: Harry N. Abrams, 1966. This treasure of a book—with its silk binding and tipped-in illustrations—offers a clear and detailed introduction to all forms of ikebana.

Serrell, Migi. *The Art of Arranging Flowers*. Manchester City, Vermont: Golden Quill Press, 1997. The author leads the reader through simple arrangements to exhibiting in flower shows. An encouraging book from an arranger with decades of experience.

Skinner, Helen. *The Canadian Flower Arranger*. Toronto: Macmillan Canada, 1993. Traditional and modern designs by Canadian flower arrangers appear in this commemorative book created to coincide with the World Association of Flower Arrangers Fourth World Flower Show in Ontario.

Smith, George W. *George Smith's Flower Decoration: English Classic Design*. London: Penguin Group/Mermaid Books, 1993. This well-known demonstrator gives a detailed description of the setting, plant material and mechanics of each arrangement.

Société Nationale d'Horticulture de France-Section Art Floral. *Bouquets sans fleurs, fleurir la vie, tables fleuries*. 3 vols. Paris, 2001.

———. *La France et ses Bouquets*. Paris, 1998.

———. *L'art du bouquet en France*. Paris: Armand Colin Editeur, 1993.

Sparnon, Norman. *Japanese Flower Arrangement—Classical and Modern*. Rutland, Vermont, and Tokyo: Charles E. Tuttle Company, 1960.

———. *Japanese Flower Arrangement*. Tokyo: Shufunotomo Co., 1982. The author of these two and a number of other books, Sparnon is an outstanding authority on ikebana and is credited with introducing the Western world to this Japanese art. Each beautiful arrangement is accompanied by an explanation.

Steere, Dr. William C. *Flower Arrangement: The Ikebana Way*. Tokyo: Shufunotomo Co., 1988. A history of the Japanese art of flower arranging is followed by clear instructions for adapting this art to the modern American home.

Stoltz, Mrs. Raymond Russ. *Interpretive Floral Designs*. Cranbury, New Jersey: A. S. Barnes & Co., 1972. A fine guide for the arranger who wants to better understand interpretive classes in flower shows.

Sutter, Anne Bernat. *New Approach to Design Principles: A Comprehensive Analysis of Design Elements and Principles in Floral Design*. Overland, Missouri: Sutter Publishing, 1973. This well-illustrated book leads the arranger by the hand to an understanding of how design principles apply to flower arranging.

Taylor, Jean. *Creative Flower Arrangement*. London: Stanley Paul, 1993. An invaluable source of information, ideas, and inspiration from the former editor of *The Flower Arranger*. Taylor has greatly influenced English flower arranging with this and nine other books.

Taylor, Paul. *Dutch Flower Painting, 1600-1720*. New Haven, Connecticut: Yale University Press, 1995. A scholarly exploration of the genre for the arranger fascinated by the period.

Tharp, Leonard. *An American Style of Flower Arrangement*. Dallas: Taylor Publishing Company, 1986. One of the first floral demonstrators to use weeds and grasses with beautiful flowers, shaping an American style.

Tsujii, Hoin Koshu. *The Mastery of Japanese Flower Arrangement*. Kyoto, Japan: Mitsuhana and Company, 1962. This book gives fundamental information on the Misho and Ohara schools of ikebana.

Turner, Elizabeth Hutton. *Georgia O'Keeffe: The Poetry of Things*. Washington, D. C.: The Phillips Collection, 1999. The text provides interesting insight into O'Keeffe's powers of observation and her focus on flowers.

Vagg, Daphne. *European Continental Styles*. Revised. London: National Association of Flower Arrangement Societies, 1998. A NAFAS booklet illustrating current styles—parallel, modern mass, and so forth.

van Uffelen, Aad. *Flower-World: A Road to Floral Art*. Zutphen, Holland: Terra 2001.

———. *Moderne Bloemsierkunst*. Zutphen, Holland: Terra. 1991.

van Uffelen, Aad, and Jan van der Loos. *Bloemsierkunst: Feestelijk schikken in vele stijlen en technieken*. Antwerp, Holland: Groen Boekerij,

1985. The three books listed above and others by the Dutch floral artist are inspirational eye-openers. The older two have Dutch text, but the arrangements speak for themselves.

WAFA South Africa. *Dreaming of Africa*. Umhlanga Rocks, South Africa: World Association of Flower Arrangers, South Africa, 1999. A commemorative edition of traditional and modern designs by African flower arrangers published to coincide with the WAFA meeting in Durban, South Africa.

Webb, Iris, ed. *The Complete Guide to Flower and Foliage Arrangements*. Exeter, England: Webb & Bower, 1979. This classic, compiled by a former president of National Association of Flower Arranging Societies of Great Britain, still teaches—traditional line, line-mass, and mass, to abstract and ikebana; from church flowers to show work.

Wood, June Pitts, and Deen Day Smith. *Table Settings For All Seasons in the Home and in the Flower Show*. St. Louis: National Council of State Garden Clubs, Inc. 1994. A particularly helpful guide to exhibiting in table classes in flower shows.

Publications

PERIODICALS

Periodicals devoted to the art of flower arranging are the next best thing to actually visiting a flower show or floral exhibition. Their full-color photography records new trends, and the informative texts explain techniques and equipment. They serve as the teaching instrument for the professional floral industry and for flower-arranging organizations around the world. Some of those mentioned below may be available in libraries or at florist shops, but subscription addresses are provided here.

GCA By Design
Newsletter of the Flower Arranging Study Group of the Garden Club of America. Published quarterly. To subscribe, send check for $15.00 to:
FASG—*GCA By Design*
The Garden Club of America
14 E. 60th Street
New York, NY 10022

Floral Focus
The magazine of the Floral Art Society of New Zealand, Inc., is published twice yearly. To subscribe, contact FASNZ through their Internet address: www.fasnz.org.nz

The Florist
A professional American magazine for retail florists, it is published monthly by the FTD Association as a business resource. To subscribe, send credit card information by mail to:
FTD Association—*The Florist*
33031 Schoolcraft Road
Livonia, MI 48150

The Florists' Review
This has been a trade publication of the American floral industry since 1897. Published monthly, it features a special "Sourcebook" in the June issue that lists, by state, wholesalers of fresh, tropical, and dried materials as well as schools, associations, and more. Subscribe on line at www.floristreview.com or send credit card information to:
Florists' Review
P. O. Box 4368
Topeka, KS 66604

The Flower Arranger
Insight—The Educational Journal for Flower Arrangers

These two journals are published by the National Association of Flower Arrangement Societies—United Kingdom. For more information and to subscribe online, go to www.nafas.org.uk; or fax credit card information to the distribution officer at 011-44-1704-225546; or by mail to:
Taylor Bloxham Ltd.
17-21 Tollwell Road
Bursom Industrial Estate
Beaumont Leys, Leicester LE4 1BR, England

Holland Flower
This quarterly is published by the Flower Council of Holland for floral professionals and educators. To subscribe, contact:
Flower Council of Holland
250 West 57th Street
New York, NY 10019

PFD– Professional Floral Designer
This professional publication is published six times a year "to educate and inspire the floral industry worldwide." To subscribe, send credit card information to:
American Floral Services, Inc.
3737 NW 34th Street
P. O. Box 12309
Oklahoma City, OK 73157

BOOKLETS

Clubs and individuals in the Garden Club of America have produced multiple publications related to flower shows and flower arranging. This is a way to share years of cumulative learning with new members or new converts to the art of flower arranging. Ordering information appears below; all prices include shipping and handling.

The Alphabet of the New Canaan Garden Club–1930
This fourteen-page humorous poem, written in 1930 by May Potter, has been resurrected and faithfully reprinted—from *artistic* to *zeal*. To order, send check for $6.00, payable to:
New Canaan Garden Club
c/o Catherine C. Pike
79 Indian Waters Drive
New Canaan, CT 06840

Always Cut Under Water . . .
Gail Emmons has compiled her recommendations for prolonging the life of cut plant material in floral arrangements, including pretreating, special conditioning, hardening, and preserving. To order, send check for $10.00, payable to
The Orinda Garden Club
P. O. Box 34
Orinda, CA 94563

Flowers for Bouquets: Conditioning Plant Material for Flower Arranging
Joanne Lenden provides conditioning techniques, tips, tidbits, and specific treatments for more than 400 plants, supplying both botanical and common names. To order, send check for $12.95, payable to:
Joanne Lenden
223 Westchester Drive
Delmar, NY 12054

Gardening for Southern Seasons
This guide to gardening practices in the American South is arranged by seasons. To order, send check for $17.00, payable to:
The Monroe Garden Study League
P. O. Box 2152
Monroe, LA 71207

Keep Fresh Things Fresh
This compilation of wisdom from clubs, speakers, and the Filoli Garden Shop on how to extend the life of plant material is alphabetically arranged by plant type. To order, send a check for $9.00, payable to:
Seattle Garden Club
University of Washington
Center for Urban Horticulture
Box 354115
Seattle, WA 98195

The Ministry of Flowers
Lucy Manson, a twenty-four-year veteran of church flower arrangements, gives hints, tricks, and caveats as a primer for anyone approaching this specialized subject. To order, send a check for $6.00, payable to:
Lucy Manson
4600 Middleton Park Circle East #D344
Jacksonville, FL 32224

Petal Perfect
Alphabetically organized, from Agapanthus to Zinnia, this booklet details specific cutting, conditioning, and hardening procedures for flowers and foliage. To order, send a check for $8.00, payable to:
Garden Club of Darien
Box 1213
Darien, CT 06820

Styles of Flower Arranging–A Primer
Sketches help arrangers execute historical styles of arrangements, starting with sixteenth-century European flower pieces through contemporary designs. To order, send a check for $6.00, payable to:
The Elizabeth River Garden Club
P. O. Box 7923
Portsmouth, VA 23707

Three Hundred Years of Flower Arranging in America
Forty arrangements, chronicling American flower arranging from 1620 to 1998, were photographed at the 1998 Annual Meeting

Flower Show of the Garden Club of America in Williamsburg, Virginia. This full-color, special edition of the *Flower Arranging Study Group Newsletter* was produced by Penny Horne and includes judges' comments, as well as the botanical and common names of the plant material in the arrangements. To order, send check for $10.00, payable to:
FASG of GCA
Garden Club of America
14 East 60th Street
New York, NY 10022

Tips for Exhibiting in Flower Shows–4th Edition
Experienced Philadelphia Flower Show participants offer tips on exhibiting in both flower arranging and horticulture classes—touching on rules, tools, goals, lighting, transporting challenges, and more. To order send a check for $9.00, payable to P.C.G.C.A., to:
Gretchen Riley
526 Avonwood Road
Haverford, PA 19041

What's in a Name?
Mary S. Wooster demystifies Latin and Greek nomenclature in this beginner's guide to the botanical names of plants. To order, send request to:
The Garden Club of Montclair, Inc.
60 S. Fullerton Avenue
Montclair, NJ 07042

SOURCES FOR FLOWER-ARRANGING BOOKS

Where can arrangers find flower-arranging books—foreign and domestic, new and out of print? The following companies specialize in this market and have proved valuable sources. The first five booksellers offer book search as a service without obligation:

American Botanist
Keith Crotz
1103 W. Truitt Avenue
Chillicothe, IL 61523
agbook@mtco.com
309-274-5254

Book Barn Ltd.
17 Market Place
Glastonbury SOM
United Kingdom BA69HL
011-441-749-676162
bookbarn@netcomuk.co.uk

Britton Booksellers
2110 Lockhaven Drive
Colorado Springs, CO 80909
brttnbooks@aol.com

C. C. Saladino Booksellers
P. O. Box 3462
Dana Point, CA 92629
sales@oldbooksforsale.com
949-488-0692

Considine Books
P. O. Box 395
Marlborough, CT 06447
jfconsidine@snet.net
888-297-2665 (Toll free)

European Floral Design Library
513 West Campbell Road
Richardson, TX 75080
972-234-6017
Uta Snetzlinger has assembled a collection
of serious foreign flower-arranging books.
Orders may take several weeks.

Flower Arranging Study Group
The Garden Club of America
14 East 60th Street
New York, NY 10022
212-753-0134
www.gcamerica.org
The Flower Arranging Study Group buys
just-released flower-arranging books, mostly
by foreign designers, in volume for resale
distribution.

McLeods Booksellers Limited of Rotorua
1217 Hinemoa Street
Rotorua, Tauranga, New Zealand
mcleods@clear.net.nz
Fax 011-64-7-349-0288
This much-respected vendor carries a wide
range of international flower-arranging books
and will ship anywhere in the world. Contact
them for inclusion on their mailing list.

NAFAS Enterprises Ltd.—The Book Secretary
Osborne House
12 Devonshire Square
London EC2M 4TE England
www.nafas.org.uk
Check the website for a comprehensive list of
booklets and flower-arranging books, including
the NAFAS Judges and Competitors Manual and
NAFAS Show Guide.

Powell's City of Books
3747 S. E. Hawthorne Boulevard
Portland, OR 97214
800-354-5957
Fax 503-230-7112
www.powells.com
The inventory of eight stores is on the web,
including a special store for cooks and gardeners
(address above). Powell's will hold your request
until they are able to fill it.

The Royal Horticultural Society—England
www.rhs.org.uk
The Royal Horticultural Society has many
informative publications available for export,
including the RHS Show Handbook.

Titles, Inc.
Florence Shay, Proprietor
1931 Sheridan Road
Highland Park, IL 60035
847 432-3690
This dealer in rare and valuable books offers
a search service.

The Trellis Shop, Civic Garden Centre
777 Lawrence Avenue, East
Toronto, Ontario
Canada M3C 1P2
416-397-1340
cgc@civicgardencentre.org
Cathie Cox, horticulturalist and shop manager,
is the person to contact for flower-arranging
books and supplies. Will ship anywhere.

FLOWER-ARRANGING INSTRUCTION

Books, booklets, and periodicals can certainly
inspire and teach, but at some point the
arranger will want more formal instruction.
Check with local botanical gardens, garden
centers, colleges and universities. For professional
flower-arranging schools in your area, consult
the June issue of The Florists' Review (see
Periodicals).

When person-to-person teaching is not
possible, a video course may prove to be a
desirable option. Two instructional videos by
the Reverend William McMillan of Belfast,
Northern Ireland, are recent favorites—Rev. Mac:
A Man for All Seasons and Mac II. To order, contact:

Markelly Vision
P. O. Box XV
Crumlin BT29 4GL Northern Ireland

Many other domestic and foreign flower-
arranging videos are available for rental or
purchase. Check your local library, video supplier,
the sponsoring organization, or search the
Internet. Videos are often produced in connection with flower shows, such as the WAFA World
Flower Shows, New Zealand's Floravision, and
many U.S. shows, including the Philadelphia
Flower Show and the Memphis Flower Show.

The National Association of Flower
Arranging Societies in Great Britain (NAFAS)
offers a diploma in floral art and design in a
home-study course for overseas students. The
course begins with an introduction to the art of
designing with plant material, continues with a
discussion of the concepts and techniques
involved, and moves through a broad-based,
complete flower-arranging education. The
home-study section is followed by a residential
course of one week in the U.K., for assessment
and verification. Check the website at
www.nafas.org.uk or contact:

NAFAS Education Secretary
Osborne House
12 Devonshire Square
London EC2M 4TE England

appendix G Glossary of Flower-Arranging Terms

abstract: A contemporary design style characterized by boldness, space, and interest distributed throughout the design. Plant material and other components are used for their design qualities—line, form, color, and texture.

arrangement: Plant material and other components—including container, base, and background—organized according to the principles of design to create a unified whole. *Arrangement, composition,* and *design* are used synonymously.

balance: Actual and apparent stability in a design, which should be evident from side to side, front to back, and top to bottom. In other words, an arrangement should not appear ready to fall on its face or topple over backward or sideways.

base: A component used under the container or arrangement; it can add weight to the lower part of the design and affect balance.

complementary colors: Two colors that lie opposite or close to opposite each other on the color wheel and therefore create the most dramatic contrasts, e.g., red and green, orange and blue, yellow and violet.

component: One of the parts that makes up a design—plant material, container, mechanics, background, base, and so forth.

contemporary design: Any style in current or recent fashion as opposed to traditional and period designs. Current contemporary styles include parallel, abstract, freestyle, and modern mass.

contrast: A design element that adds interest to an arrangement by emphasizing the differences of texture, color, and form.

dominance: A design principle closely related to contrast. Contrast offers interest and variety, but one element—color, texture, line, form—must dominate in order to achieve unity.

elements of design: The ingredients or qualities found in plant material and other components—color, line, form, texture, pattern, size, space.

focal area: Dominant point in a design to which the eye is first drawn before moving through the rest of the design. Too strong a focal area stops the movement, creating a bull's-eye.

form: The three-dimensional contour of a design or of individual components. The form of a flower might be open as in a tulip or closed as in a rosebud. The form of an arrangement might be cone-shaped and closed, as in the Byzantine design, or open as in many ikebana and abstract designs.

frame of reference: Similar to the background of a design or the space available to the arranger.

freestyle: A term applied to the freedom of expression in twentieth- and twenty-first-century designs as they contrast with the traditional and classic ikebana designs. It indicates a freedom for the arranger to design in any nontraditional style.

interpretive design: An arrangement in which components have been selected and organized to portray a theme or idea.

line: The two-dimensional quality of plant material, such as branches; also, the main direction of movement or the primary visual path through a design.

line arrangement: A design in which line is the dominant element, usually with an open silhouette and a limited amount of plant material, as in many traditional ikebana designs.

line mass arrangement: A design in which the line is reinforced by a mass of plant material; usually asymmetrical with a rhythmic flow.

mass arrangement: A design style with a profusion of plant material arranged in a closed silhouette with few or no voids.

massed line: A style in which mass is prominent, but there is significant line direction, as in the flowing S of a Hogarth curve.

mechanics: Devices that help to support plant material in a design, including pin holders, Oasis, chicken wire, floral tape, wire, and so forth.

modern mass: A contemporary European style in which a mass of one variety of plant material is juxtaposed with another mass to create bold contrasts in color, texture, and form.

moribana: An ikebana term for a style arranged in a low, flat container. Plant material is usually held in place in a kenzan, or pinholder.

monochromatic design: An arrangement in which all components are in the tints, tones, and shades of one hue.

nageire: An ikebana term for a style that is arranged in tall vases or baskets, often a line arrangement.

niche: In flower shows, staging that is enclosed on three sides, often recessed into a wall, with lighting from above.

parallel: A contemporary style in which groupings of plant material are arranged at regular intervals with space in between and often connective material at the base.

pattern: A design element referring to the silhouette—including solids and spaces—of an arrangement or a component as seen against a background.

pavé: In jewelry making a term that refers to setting stones so close together that no metal shows. In flower arranging pavé is a technique of placing groups of plant material that have been cut very short close together to form undulating mounds of colors, textures, shapes, and sizes. Any plant material—flowers, foliage, cut stems, fruits, vegetables, mushrooms, moss—can be used.

period arrangements: Designs with characteristics similar to those favored during an historic period.

proportion: A design principle that refers to the relationship of one portion of the design to the whole or to another portion—the amount of plant material to the container, for example. *Too much* or *too little* will refer to proportion.

rhythm: A design principle referring to the movement or the visual path the eye follows through a design, usually achieved by repetition and line direction.

rikka: A standing ikebana style characterized by the trunklike placement of plant material that rises above the waterline.

scale: Refers to the size relationship of individual components to one another, such as the size of the individual flower to the container. Scale is particularly important in miniature designs. *Too small* or *too big* will refer to scale.

space: A design element that refers to the voids in the design and the space contained in the plant material as well as the space in which the design is staged.

still life: A composition of plant material and other components chosen for their design qualities and the story they tell.

synergistic design: A contemporary style in which several containers are used in a composition. Each container may hold a complete or a partial arrangement as long as the combined units create a unified whole.

tables—exhibition: A class in flower shows in which the components—dishes, plant material, linen, accessories—are arranged artistically to present a coordinated design. No service of food is implied.

tables—functional: A class in flower shows in which the table is arranged for the service of food.

traditional mass arrangement: A style of design characterized by a profusion of plant material arranged in a closed silhouette with few or no voids.

unity: A goal of flower arranging; to organize the components into a harmonious whole.

Photography notes and credits

Page 2, Julie Lapham, Southborough, Massachusetts; Worcester Garden Club, Zone I. Photographed at Tower Hill Botanic Garden, Boylston, Massachusetts, June 2001.

Page 5, Gail Emmons, Orinda, California; Orinda Garden Club, Zone XII. Photographed at Filoli, Woodside, California, May 2001.

Page 6, Elvira M. Butz, Winnetka, Illinois; Garden Guild of Winnetka, Zone XI. Photographed at "Show of Summer," a GCA Major Flower Show held at the Chicago Botanic Garden, Glencoe, Illinois, June 2000.

Page 9, Phoebe Kahl and Diana Rupp-Kennedy; Orinda, California. Orinda Garden Club. Originally exhibited at "Visions," a GCA Major Flower Show. Re-created and photographed at Filoli, Woodside, California, May 2001.

Page 10, Cecile McCaull, Greenwich, Connecticut; Hortulus, Zone II. Photographed June 2001.

Section One. Our Flower-Arranging Heritage

Page 13, Manisse K. Newell, Hillsborough, California; Hillsborough Garden Club, Zone XII. Photographed at Filoli, Woodside, California, May 2001.

Chapter 1. Flower Arranging in the West—A Very Long Tradition

Page 19, Lou Greer, Santa Barbara, California; Garden Club of Santa Barbara, Zone XII. Photographed at Filoli, Woodside, California, May 2001.

Page 20, Carolyn Musto, San Mateo, California; Hillsborough Garden Club, Zone XII. Photographed at Filoli, Woodside, California, May 2001.

Page 21, Ellie Gardner, Portola Valley, California; Woodside-Atherton Garden Club, Zone XII. Photographed at Filoli, Woodside, California, May 2001.

Page 22, Margaret Lee Blunt, Burlingame, California; Hillsborough Garden Club, Zone XII. Photographed at Filoli, Woodside, California, May 2001.

Pages 23, 24, Carol Ballard and Laura Wheless, Houston, Texas; River Oaks Garden Club, Zone IX. Photographed at Bayou Bend, Museum of Fine Arts, Houston, April 2001.

Page 25, Cary Lide, Atlanta, Georgia; Peachtree Garden Club, Zone VIII. Photographed at Rienzi, Museum of Fine Arts, Houston, April 2001.

Page 26, Diane Dalton, Chestnut Hill, Massachusetts; Chestnut Hill Garden Club, Zone I. Kitty Ferguson, Westwood, Massachusetts; Fox Hill Garden Club, Zone I. Originally exhibited at New England Flower Show, Boston. Re-created and photographed at Tower Hill Botanic Garden, Boylston, Massachusetts, June 2001.

Page 27, Martha Newton Law, Lookout Mountain, Tennessee; Garden Club of Lookout Mountain, Zone IX. Photographed at the Hunt and Polo Club, Memphis, Tennessee, April 2000.

Page 28, Anne Helfert, San Mateo, California; Hillsborough Garden Club, Zone XII. Photographed at Filoli, Woodside, California, May 2001.

Page 29, Elizabeth Ann Bunce, Portland, Oregon; Portland Garden Club, Zone XII. Photographed at "Inspirations 2001," a Garden Club of America Major Flower Show sponsored by the Portland Garden Club and held at the Portland Art Museum, April 2001.

Page 30, Bertie Lee, Honolulu, Hawaii; Garden Club of Honolulu, Zone XII. Photographed at the home of Claire and Larry Johnson, Honolulu, April 2001.

Page 31, Ann S. Stevens, Savannah, Georgia; Trustees' Garden Club, Zone VIII. Photographed at the home of Ann and John Tatum, Savannah, Zone VIII meeting, April 2000.

Page 31, Liz Farnsworth, Memphis, Tennessee; Memphis Garden Club, Zone IX. Photographed at home of Liz and Tommy Farnsworth, Memphis, April 2000.

Chapter 2. Ikebana—Ancient Art, Newest Influence

Page 35, This *rikka* was created for "Art en Fleurs," a GCA Major Show held at the Milwaukee Art Museum in August 2001, as part of an exhibition of ikebana styles. Maribeth Price, professor of ikebana and member of Kettle Moraine Garden Club in Wisconsin, staged the exhibition, which included arrangements by her students and associates, two of whom—Professor Kimiko Gunji and Jeanne Holy—built this *rikka*.

Page 36, Maribeth Price, Hartland, Wisconsin; Kettle Moraine Garden Club, Zone XI. Photographed at the Memphis Botanic Garden, Memphis, Tennessee, April 2000.

Pages 37, 38, 39, Jane Morgan, Rydall, Pennsylvania; Huntingdon Valley Garden Club, Zone V. Photographed by Jane Morgan.

Page 40, Gail Emmons, Orinda, California; Orinda Garden Club, Zone XII. Photographed at Filoli, Woodside, California, May 2001.

Page 41, Dorothy W. Elliott, Cleveland Heights, Ohio; Shaker Lakes Garden Club, Zone X. Photographed at the home of Jane and Bob Pinkas, Cleveland Heights, April 2000.

Page 42, Jane Morgan, Rydall, Pennsylvania; Huntingdon Valley Garden Club, Zone V. Photographed by Jane Morgan.

Page 43, Asta Johnson, Carmel, California; Woodside-Atherton Garden Club, Zone XII. Photographed at Filoli, Woodside, California, May 2001.

Page 44, Kay Cobb and Susan Harrison, Savannah, Georgia; Trustees' Garden Club, Zone VIII. Photographed at the home of Audrey and Dick Platt, Savannah, Zone VIII meeting, April 2000.

of America, Cleveland, Ohio, April 2000. We are grateful to the show chairman, Bliss Clark, Garden Club of Michigan, and her committee for their inspiring schedule and invaluable assistance in photographing these designs.

Page 91, Julie Lapham, Southborough, Massachusetts; Worcester Garden Club, Zone I.

Page 92, Lou Greer, Santa Barbara, California; Garden Club of Santa Barbara, Zone XII. The arrangement was originally designed for a flower show held at the Music Academy of the West, Santa Barbara. Re-created and photographed at Filoli, Woodside, California, May 2001.

Page 93, Maryjo Garre, Barrington, Illinois; Garden Club of Barrington, Zone XI.

Page 94, Catherine Beattie, Greenville, South Carolina; Carolina Foothills Garden Club, Zone VIII.

Page 95, Melinda Earle, Naples, Florida; Garden Club of Michigan, Zone X.

Page 96, Prudence Hammett, Yarrow Point, Washington; Seattle Garden Club, Zone XII.

Page 97, Gail Emmons, Orinda, California; Orinda Garden Club, Zone XII. Photographed at Filoli, Woodside, California, May 2001.

Page 98, Elvira M. Butz, Winnetka, Illinois; Garden Guild of Winnetka, Zone XI. Photographed at "Show of Summer," a GCA Major Flower Show held at the Chicago Botanic Garden, Glencoe, Illinois, June 2000.

Page 99, Jane Godshalk, Haverford, Pennsylvania; Four Counties Garden Club, Zone V.

Page 100, Martha N. McClellan, Knoxville, Tennessee; Knoxville Garden Club, Zone IX.

Page 101. Sherran Blair, New Albany, Ohio; Little Garden Club of Columbus, Zone X. Photographed at "Florescence", a GCA Major Flower Show held at the Museum of Fine Arts, Houston, Texas, April 2001.

Page 101, Sandra S. Baylor, Virginia Beach, Virginia; Virginia Beach Garden Club and Garden Club of Norfolk, Zone VII.

Page 102, Carol F. Critchlow, Hopewell, New Jersey; Garden Club of Trenton, Zone IV.

Page 103, Ingrid Kelly, Houston, Texas; Garden Club of Houston, Zone IX.

Page 104, Nancy Ladd, Rye, New York; Rye Garden Club, Zone III.

Page 105, Leontine LaPointe, Vero Beach, Florida; Garden Club of Nashville, Zone IX.

Page 106, Bonny Martin, Memphis, Tennessee; Memphis Garden Club, Zone IX.

Page 107, Tricia Saul, Chevy Chase, Maryland; Garden Club of Chevy Chase, Zone VI.

Page 108, Bobbie Slater and Leslie Mattice, Honolulu, Hawaii, Garden Club of Honolulu, Zone XII. Photographed at "Hawaii Calls," a GCA Major Flower Show held at the Honolulu Academy of Arts, April 2001.

Page 109, Barbara Masumoto and Dotty Nitta, Honolulu, Hawaii; Garden Club of Honolulu, Zone XII. Photographed at "Hawaii Calls," a GCA Major Flower Show, sponsored by the Garden Club of Honolulu and held at the Honolulu Academy of Arts, April 2001.

Page 109, Angeline F. Austin, Princeton, New Jersey; Stony Brook Garden Club, Zone IV.

Page 110, Claire Ellis, Savannah, Georgia; Trustees' Garden Club, Zone VIII.

Page 111, Gail Emmons, Orinda, California; Orinda Garden Club, Zone XII. Photographed at Filoli, Woodside, California, May 2001.

Page 112, Margaret Pengilly, Piedmont, California; Piedmont Garden Club, Zone XII. Photographed at Filoli, Woodside, California, May 2001.

Page 113, Susan Detjens, Sheffield, Massachusetts; Garden Club of Wilmington, Zone V.

Page 114, Nancy D'Oench, Portland, Connecticut; Middletown Garden Club, Zone II.

Page 115, Sally Humphreys, Wyndmoor, Pennsylvania; Huntingdon Valley Garden Club, Zone V.

Page 116, Margaret Pengilly, Piedmont, California; Piedmont Garden Club, Zone XII. Originally created for a Piedmont Garden Club Flower Show. Re-created and photographed at Filoli, Woodside, California, May 2001.

Page 117, Patsy L. Gibson, Waialua, Hawaii, and Pat Schnack, Honolulu, Hawaii; Garden Club of Honolulu, Zone XII. Photographed at "Hawaii Calls," a GCA Major Flower Show, held at the Honolulu Academy of Arts, April 2001.

Page 118, Anna Lise Dyhr Vogel and Bertie Lee, Honolulu, Hawaii; Garden Club of Honolulu, Zone XII. Photographed at "Hawaii Calls," a GCA Major Flower Show, held at the Honolulu Academy of Arts, April 2001.

Page 119, Tad Sewell and Sally Moore, Honolulu, Hawaii; Garden Club of Honolulu, Zone XII. Photographed at "Hawaii Calls," a GCA Major Flower Show, held at the Honolulu Academy of Arts, April 2001.

Page 120, Cynthia Affleck and Anna Smith, Wyndmoor, Pennsylvania; Wissahickon Garden Club, Zone V. Photographed at the Philadelphia Flower Show, Philadelphia, Pennsylvania, March 2000.

Pages 120, 121, Bonnie Schorsch and Shelley Schorsch, Meadowbrook, Pennsylvania; Huntingdon Valley Garden Club, Zone V. Photographed at the Philadelphia Flower Show, March 2000.

Page 122, Tanya Alston, Kailua, Hawaii, and Ele Potts, Honolulu, Hawaii; Garden Club of Honolulu, Zone XII. Photographed at "Hawaii Calls," a GCA Major Flower Show, held at the Honolulu Academy of Arts, April 2001.

Page 123, Kathy Powell, Hopewell, New Jersey; designed and chaired this exhibit, an entry in the Room Class at the Philadelphia Flower Show by the Garden Club of Trenton, Zone IV. Photographed at the Philadelphia Flower Show, Philadelphia, Pennsylvania, March 2001.

Chapter 7. Floral Fashions—Botanic Couture

Page 124, Isabel Morian Lamb, Beaumont, Texas; Magnolia Garden Club of Beaumont, Zone IX. Photographed at "Florescence," a GCA Major Flower Show, held at the Museum of Fine Arts, Houston, Texas, April 2001.

Page 125, Nancy Godshall, Houston, Texas; Garden Club of Houston, Zone IX. Photographed at "Florescence," a GCA Major Flower Show held at the Museum of Fine Arts, Houston, April 2001.

Page 125, Ann Heist, Ormond Beach, Florida; Garden Club of the Halifax Country, Zone VIII. Photographed at "Florescence," a GCA Major

Flower Show, held at the Museum of Fine Arts, Houston, Texas, April 2001.

Page 126, Sally Chapman and Mari Tischenko, Orinda, California; Orinda Garden Club, Zone XII. Photographed at Filoli, Woodside, California, May 2001.

Page 127, Sally Chapman, Orinda, California; Orinda Garden Club; Ellie Gardner, Portola Valley, California; Woodside–Atherton Garden Club; and Mari Tischenko, Orinda, California; Orinda Garden Club, Zone XII. Photographed at Filoli, Woodside, California, May 2001.

Page 128, Jane Kilduff, Philadelphia, Pennsylvania; Wissahickon Garden Club, Zone V. Photographed at the Philadelphia Flower Show, March 2001.

Page 129, Julie Lapham, Southborough, Massachusetts; Worcester Garden Club, Zone I. Originally exhibited at a flower show sponsored by the Nantucket Garden Club. Re-created and photographed at Tower Hill Botanic Garden, Boylston, Massachusetts, June 2001.

Page 130, Alice Hamilton Farley, Philadelphia, Pennsylvania; Wissahickon Garden Club, Zone V. Photographed at the Philadelphia Flower Show, Philadelphia, Pennsylvania, March 2000.

Page 131, Ginny Simonin, Wyndmoor, Pennsylvania; Wissahickon Garden Club, Zone V. Photographed at the Philadelphia Flower Show, Philadelphia, Pennsylvania, March 2000.

Page 132, Jane Vanderzee, New Canaan, Connecticut; New Canaan Garden Club, Zone II. Photographed at the Philadelphia Flower Show, Philadelphia, Pennsylvania, March 2000.

Page 133, Dottie Sheffield, Wyndmoor, Pennsylvania; Newport Garden Club, Zone II. Photographed at the Philadelphia Flower Show, Philadelphia, Pennsylvania, March 2000.

Page 133, Betty Davis, Houston, Texas; Garden Club of Houston, Zone IX. Photographed at "Florescence," a GCA Major Flower Show, held at the Museum of Fine Arts, Houston, April 2001.

Chapter 8. Museums—Fine Art with Flowers

Page 135, Cathie Pike and Cecilie Cruger, New Canaan, Connecticut; New Canaan Garden Club, Zone II. Photographed at "Fine Art and Flowers," Wadsworth Atheneum, Hartford,

Connecticut, April 2001. **Art credit:** Jacopo Robusti, called Il Tintoretto. *The Contest Between Apollo and Marsyas.* The Wadsworth Atheneum Museum of Art. The Ella Gallup Sumner and Mary Catllin Sumner Collection Fund.

Page 136, Lucy Belding, Tucson, Arizona; Garden Study Club of New Orleans, Zone IX. Photographed at "Florescence," a GCA Major Flower Show, held at the Museum of Fine Arts, Houston, Texas, April 2001. **Art credit:** Roman Artist. *Standing Figure of a Goddess.* The Museum of Fine Arts, Houston. Gift of Mr. and Mrs. John J. Moran.

Page 136, Nina Hayssen, Hartland, Wisconsin; Kettle Moraine Garden Club, Zone XI. Photographed at "Art en Fleurs," a GCA Major Flower Show, held at the Milwaukee Art Museum, Milwaukee, Wisconsin, August 2001. **Art credit:** Francesco Solimena. *Madonna and Child with Saints Januarius and Sebastian.* Milwaukee Art Museum.

Page 137, Sheila Graham-Smith, Middletown, Connecticut; Middletown Garden Club, Zone II. Photographed at "Fine Art and Flowers," Wadsworth Atheneum, Hartford, Connecticut, April 2001. **Art credit:** François Boucher. *The Eggseller.* The Wadsworth Atheneum Museum of Art. The Ella Gallup Sumner and Mary Catllin Sumner Collection Fund.

Page 138, Judith Stark, Nashotah, Wisconsin; Kettle Moraine Garden Club, Zone XI. Photographed at "Art en Fleurs," a GCA Major Flower Show, held at the Milwaukee Art Museum, Milwaukee, Wisconsin, August 2001. **Art credit:** Nardo di Cione. *Madonna and Child.* Milwaukee Art Museum.

Page 139, Cato Schley, Fox Point, Wisconsin; Green Tree Garden Club, Zone XI. Photographed at "Art en Fleurs," a GCA Major Flower Show, held at the Milwaukee Art Museum, Milwaukee, Wisconsin, August 2001. **Art credit:** Jean-Léon Gérôme. *The Two Majesties.* Milwaukee Art Museum.

Page 140, Laura Gregg, Bryn Mawr, Pennsylvania; the Garden Workers; and Lani McCall, Philadelphia, Pennsylvania; Garden Club of Philadelphia, Zone V. Photographed at "Florescence," a GCA Major Flower Show, held at the Museum of Fine Arts, Houston, Texas, April 2001. **Art credit:** Frederic Remington. *The Herd Boy.* The Museum of Fine Arts, Houston. The Hogg Brothers Collection, gift of Miss Ima Hogg.

Page 141, Bonny Martin, Memphis, Tennessee; Memphis Garden Club, Zone IX. Photographed at "Flowers and Art," a GCA Major Flower Show held at the Dixon Gallery and Gardens, Memphis, April 2000. **Art credit:** Botanical art from the Shirley Sherwood Collection.

Page 142, Margot Paddock, Pittsfield, Massachusetts; Berkshire Garden Club, Zone I. Photographed at "Flowers and Art," a GCA Major Flower Show held at the Dixon Gallery and Gardens, Memphis, Tennessee, April 2000. **Art credit:** Botanical art from the Shirley Sherwood Collection.

Page 143, Helen Goddard, South Dartmouth, Massachusetts; Garden Club of Buzzards Bay, Zone I. Photographed at "Flowers and Art," a GCA Major Flower Show held at the Dixon Gallery and Gardens, Memphis, Tennessee, April 2000. **Art credit:** Botanical art from the Shirley Sherwood Collection.

Page 144, Jenny Lynn Bradley and Claire Ellis, Savannah, Georgia; Trustees' Garden Club, Zone VIII. Photographed at "Flowers and Art," a GCA Major Flower Show held at the Dixon Gallery and Gardens, Memphis, Tennessee, April 2000. **Art credit:** Botanical art from the Shirley Sherwood Collection.

Page 145, Maryjo Garre, Barrington, Illinois; Garden Club of Barrington, Zone XI. Photographed at "Art en Fleurs," a GCA Major Flower Show, held at the Milwaukee Art Museum, Milwaukee, Wisconsin, August 2001. **Art credit:** Barbara Hepworth. *Two Piece Marble.* Milwaukee Art Museum.

Page 146, Nancy D'Oench, Portland, Connecticut; Middletown Garden Club, Zone II. Photographed at "Fine Art and Flowers," Wadsworth Atheneum, Hartford, Connecticut, April 2001. **Art credit:** Oskar Schlemmer. *Race (Wettlauf).* The Wadsworth Atheneum Museum of Art. Gift of Philip Johnson.

Page 147, Nancy Ladd, Rye, New York; Rye Garden Club, Zone III. Photographed at "Fine Art and Flowers," Wadsworth Atheneum, Hartford, Connecticut, April 2001. **Art credit:** René Magritte. *Les Intermittences du Coeur (The Fickleness of the Heart).* The Wadsworth Atheneum Museum of Art. Gift of Tanaquil Le Clerq and George Balanchine. © 2002 C. Herscovici, Brussels/Artists Rights Society (ARS), New York.

Page 148, Penny Horne, Barrington, Illinois; Garden Club of Barrington, Zone XI. Originally exhibited at "Flowers and Art," a GCA Major Flower Show held at the Dixon Gallery and Gardens, Memphis, Tennessee. Re-created and photographed at "Fine Art and Flowers," Wadsworth Atheneum, Hartford, Connecticut, April 2001. **Art credit:** Nancy Cheairs. *Procession.* Private Collection.

Page 149, Margot Paddock, Pittsfield, Massachusetts; Berkshire Garden Club, Zone I. Photographed at "Florescence," a GCA Major Flower Show, held at the Museum of Fine Arts, Houston, Texas, April 2001. Art credit: Jackson Pollock. *Number 6.* The Museum of Fine Arts, Houston. Museum purchase with funds provided by D. and J. de Menil. © The Pollock-Krasner Foundation/ Artists Rights Society (ARS), New York.

Page 149, Gay Estes, Houston, Texas; Garden Club of Houston, Zone IX. Photographed at "Art en Fleurs," a GCA Major Flower Show, held at the Milwaukee Art Museum, Milwaukee, Wisconsin, August 2001. **Art credit:** Roy Lichtenstein. *Crying Girl.* Milwaukee Art Museum.

Page 150, Carol Swift, Chicago, Illinois; Lake Forest Garden Club, Zone XI. Photographed at "Florescence," a GCA Major Flower Show, held at the Museum of Fine Arts, Houston, Texas, April 2001. **Art credit:** Stuart Davis. *Gloucester Harbor.* The Museum of Fine Arts, Houston. Museum purchase with funds provided by the Agnes Cullen Arnold Endowment Fund. © Estate of Stuart Davis/Licensed by VAGA, New York.

Page 151, Sylvia Abbott, Litchfield, Connecticut; Litchfield Garden Club, Zone II. Photographed at "Fine Art and Flowers," Wadsworth Atheneum, Hartford, Connecticut, April 2001. **Art credit:** Dawoud Bey. *Lakeisha, Jackie and Crystal.* The Wadsworth Atheneum Museum of Art. Gift exchange through funds from the Larsen Fund for Photography.

Page 152, Kate Coley, Hartford, Connecticut; Middletown Garden Club, Zone II. Photographed at "Fine Art and Flowers," Wadsworth Atheneum, Hartford, Connecticut, April 2001. **Art credit:** Sol LeWitt. *Wall Drawing #612.* The Wadsworth Atheneum Museum of Art. Gift of Carol and Sol LeWitt. © 2002 Sol LeWitt/Artists Rights Society (ARS), New York.

Page 153, Betty Ho, Honolulu, Hawaii; Garden Club of Honolulu, Zone XII. Photographed at "Hawaii Calls," a GCA Major Flower Show, held at the Honolulu Academy of Arts, April 2001.

Chapter 9. Beyond the Walls—New Locations, Fresh Looks

Page 155, Carol H. Henderson, Seattle, Washington; Seattle Garden Club, Zone XII. Originally exhibited in Zone XII workshop. Re-created and photographed in Las Vegas, Nevada, October 2000.

Page 156, Carol Swift, Chicago, Illinois; Lake Forest Garden Club, Zone XI. Originally exhibited at "Show of Summer," a GCA Major Flower Show held at Chicago Botanic Garden, Glencoe, Illinois. Re-created and photographed at the Museum of Fine Arts, Houston, Texas, April 2001.

Page 157, Ann Bucknall, Greenwich, Connecticut; Hortulus; and Joy Nichols, Guilford, Connecticut; Garden Club of New Haven, Zone II. Originally exhibited at the New England Flower Show, Boston, Massachusetts. Re-created and photographed in the garden of Cecile and Phil McCaull, Greenwich, Connecticut, June 2001.

Page 158, Clover Earl, White Bear Lake, Minnesota; St. Paul Garden Club, Zone XI. Originally exhibited at a flower show sponsored by the St. Paul Garden Club. Re-created and photographed at Museum of Fine Arts, Houston, April 2001.

Page 159, Carol E. McDonald, Monroe, Louisiana; Monroe Garden Study League, Zone IX. Originally exhibited at the Garden Club of America Annual Meeting Flower Show in Williamsburg,Virginia. Re-created and photographed at Graceland, Memphis, Tennessee, April 2000. Courtesy of Elvis Presley Enterprises.

Page 160, Susan Detjens, Ashley Falls, Massachusetts; and Pinkie Roe, Mendenhall, Pennsylvania; Garden Club of Wilmington, Zone V. Originally created for the Philadelphia Flower Show. Re-created and photographed at the home of Cecile and Phil McCaull, Greenwich, Connecticut, June 2001.

Page 161, Carol H. Henderson, Seattle, Washington; Seattle Garden Club, Zone XII. Originally exhibited in an in-club show. Re-created and photographed in Las Vegas, Nevada, October 2000.

Pages 162, 163, Gail Emmons, Orinda, California; Orinda Garden Club, Zone XII. Photographed at Filoli, Woodside, California, May 2001.

Page 164, Helen Goddard, South Dartmouth, Massachusetts; Garden Club of Buzzards Bay, Zone I. Photographed at Tower Hill Botanic Garden, Boylston, Massachusetts, June 2001.

Page 165, Nancy D'Oench, Portland, Connecticut; Middletown Garden Club, Zone II. Photographed at Tower Hill Botanic Garden, Boylston, Massachusetts, June 2001.

Page166, Sandra Patterson, Portola Valley, California; Woodside-Atherton Garden Club, Zone XII. Originally exhibited in a flower show sponsored by the Woodside-Atherton Garden Club. Re-created and photographed at Filoli, Woodside, California, May 2001.

Page 167, Arabella S. Dane, Boston, Massachusetts; North Shore Garden Club, Zone I. Originally exhibited at the New England Flower Show, Boston. Re-created and photographed in the garden of Pauline and Joe Runkle, Manchester, Massachusetts, June 2001.

Page 167, Maryjo Garre, Barrington, Illinois; Garden Club of Barrington, Zone XII. Originally exhibited at "Show of Summer," a GCA Major Flower Show held at the Chicago Botanic Garden, Glencoe, Illinois. Re-created and photographed at Chicago Botanic Garden, June 2000.

Pages 168, 169, Anne Crumpacker, Portland, Oregon; Portland Garden Club, Zone XII. Photographed in the garden of Anne and Jim Crumpacker, Portland, May 2001.

Pages 170, 171, Gail Emmons, Orinda, California; Orinda Garden Club, Zone XII. Photographed at Filoli, Woodside, California, May 2001.

Pages 173, 174, Photographed at Flower Arranging Study Group Workshop with instructor Carla Barbaglia, in Las Vegas, Nevada, October 2000.

Acknowledgments

CAPTURING THE MOMENT

The arrangements in this book were created by Garden Club of America members and photographed, over the course of eighteen months, by Mick Hales. Words cannot adequately express the artistic contribution this gifted photographer has made to the visual quality contained herein. Under the most difficult of circumstances—from rain-storms to crowded flower show floors—Mick found the angle, the light, and the patience to add his own art to the creations of the arrangers. For his unerring eye, his unwavering support, and his ever-gracious presence, we are grateful.

Some of the flower arrangements in this book were done on request, particularly those representing historical styles; others were recreations of designs exhibited in earlier flower shows. Most, however, were photographed at flower shows in a very limited time frame. Many factors influenced the selection, and it is far from all-inclusive. In addition to the design being in a major flower show in the eighteen-month period we were photographing, it had to be staged so that the photographer could frame a clear shot of it, with no interference from other designs, doorways, etc. In addition, it had to be a design that, regardless of how successful it was in the show, would photograph well. Bold designs photographed better than delicate; spare better than busy. The background was key to the quality—black swallowed up too much light; white could be too dominant; a patterned background such as brick confused the design. A studio setting would have made life a lot simpler but it would not have yielded the variety and spontaneity that have been captured here.

We deeply regret that we were not able to include work by many more of our accom-plished arrangers and emphasize that this is a tiny sampling of the flower arranging talent in the Garden Club of America. It is, however, an exciting introduction, one that we hope will inspire the readers' own designs and lead them to flower shows in search of still more innovative ideas.

FOR THEIR much-appreciated support of this book over the last seven years, we would like to thank the presidents of the Garden Club of America—Nancy Thomas, Jan Pratt, Chris Willemsen, Bobbie Hansen, and Ann Frierson.

For permission to photograph their homes and/or gardens, we are grateful to Jane Foster, Pauline and Joe Runkle, Cecile and Philip McCaull, Leland and Karen Miyano, Anne and Jim Crumpacker, Claire and Larry Johnson, Jane and Bob Pinkas, Audrey and Dick Platt, Emmy and Billy Winburn, Ann and John Tatum, Liz and Tommy Farnsworth, Dorothy McMillan, Posy and John Krehbiel, Howard and Mary Jo Adams, Pam and

Michael Miles, Maxine and Tom Hunter, and Pamela Armour.

We would like to thank the directors and staff of the following organizations, botanical gardens, and museums for their gracious assistance and cooperation:

The Pennsylvania Horticultural Society, sponsor of the Philadelphia Flower Show; Bayou Bend, Rienzi, and the Museum of Fine Arts, Houston; Filoli House and Gardens, Woodside, California; Dixon Gallery and Gardens, Memphis; Wadsworth Atheneum, Hartford, Connecticut; Portland Art Museum, Portland, Oregon; Milwaukee Museum of Art; Chicago Botanic Garden, Glencoe, Illinois; Honolulu Academy of Arts; Tower Hill Botanic Garden, Boylston, Massachusetts; Memphis Botanic Garden; Graceland Enterprises, Memphis; Ships of the Sea Museum, Savannah; and Dr. Shirley Sherwood for her collection of botanical prints. We also thank the Memphis Hunt and Polo Club and Bellagio, Las Vegas, for permission to photograph.

Many of the arrangements in this book were photographed at Garden Club of America major flower shows in Chicago, Honolulu, Houston, Memphis, Milwaukee, and Portland, Oregon, and at the Philadelphia Flower Show. We are grateful for the welcome and assistance offered at each event.

A very special thanks to Ms. Carla Barbaglia of Italy for permission to photograph the workshop she conducted for the Flower Arranging Study Group in Las Vegas, Nevada.

The logistics of photographing could not have been accomplished without the very valuable assistance of members across the country. We are indebted to many: Gail Emmons and Sandra Patterson for a wonderfully productive day at Filoli; Norene Alexander for preparations in Hawaii; Carol Swift for introductions in Lake Forest, Illinois; Nancy Godshall and Anne Moriniere for their assistance in Houston; Jenny Lynn Bradley for arrangements in Savannah; Diane Dalton and Julie Lapham for the day at Tower Hill Botanic Garden, Boylston, Massachusetts.

This book represents the accumulated learning of more members than we could hope to name. However, a few must be singled out. We are especially grateful to the following:

Jane Morgan for sharing her love and knowledge of ikebana;

Penny Horne for assembling a wealth of flower arranging resources and the dates and locations of flower shows across the country;

Pauline Runkle for offering her experience on conditioning;

Margot Paddock for teaching the language of welding;

Lucinda Seale for introducing us to the opportunities in the World Association of Flower Arrangers;

Ruth Crocker for her continuing leadership in the Flower Arranging Study Group;

Gay Estes for her assistance and knowledge on so many subjects, including those recorded in the Flower Arranging Study Group newsletter;

Barbara Hansen for articulating the principles of arranging and judging;

Joanne Lenden for her sleuthing in the Garden Club of America archives; and

Becky Moore for sharing her research on the history of flower shows.

To so many others who offered their help and hospitality we are grateful, especially to Frank and Juli Priebe, Carole and Ken Bailey, John Moriniere, Jim Crumpacker, Janet Dixon, John Buchanan, beloved son and daughter-in-law Montgomery and Laura Martin, and most supportive and long-suffering spouse, David B. Martin.

We would like to acknowledge John Crowley for his conviction that there was a book here; the book's designer Helene Silverman and editor Constance Herndon, who so ably coaxed images and text into a cohesive whole; and Gail Mandel whose diplomacy, efficiency, and enthusiasm led the manuscript, images, and us through the final refining stages. To Margaret Kaplan, Executive Editor and Senior Vice President, we extend our deep appreciation. Her mentoring, encouragement, and friendship have made this book possible and often a pleasure.

NANCY D'OENCH
BONNY MARTIN

I WOULD LIKE to add some very personal thanks to those who sustained me during this lengthy process.

To Elaine Carella, who on a weekly basis served as willing assistant, first respondent to text and images, and—most importantly—as good company; to Sylvia Abbott whose friendship, knowledge and perspective offered a reassuring beacon in the often confusing sea; to Penny Horne whose willingness to assist in this project never wavered, whatever the request; and to Kit Barker whose support and experience were always available and appreciated.

Any learning I have transmitted in this book has its seeds in the Middletown Garden Club. More than half a century ago member Susan Thomas wrote "The Elements and Principles of Design as They Apply to Flower Arranging." Another member, Juanie Flagg, has elucidated those principles in so many ways over the years, opening my eyes. For the club's shared talent and experience and for Juanie's mentoring, unwavering enthusiasm, and unerring sense of design, I am deeply grateful.

This project would have been abandoned long ago if it were not for the support of my family. To them I offer my love and appreciation:

To Sarah, whose own perseverance inspired me; to Susannah, whose good cheer and technical assistance were never more than a phone call away; to my sister Sue Sousa who took care of family and friends while I worked on the book; and to my dear husband Woody, who held me up and held me close during this whole endeavor.

NANCY D'OENCH

Index

Note: A plant may be known by several common names as well as by its botanical name. In the following index, italics indicate the botanical name, often widely used, and Roman letters indicate a common name. The *American Horticultural Society A-Z Encyclopedia of Garden Plants* served as a reference.